Dona Ivone Lara's Sorriso Negro

33 1/3 Global

33 1/3 Global, a series related to but independent from **33 1/3**, takes the format of the original series of short, music-based books and brings the focus to music throughout the world. With initial volumes focusing on Japanese and Brazilian music, the series will also include volumes on the popular music of Australia/Oceania, Europe, Africa, the Middle East, and more.

33 1/3 Japan

Series Editor: Noriko Manabe

Spanning a range of artists and genres—from the 1960s rock of Happy End to technopop band Yellow Magic Orchestra, the Shibuya-kei of Cornelius, classic anime series *Cowboy Bebop,* J-Pop/EDM hybrid Perfume, and vocaloid star Hatsune Miku—**33 1/3 Japan** is a series devoted to in-depth examination of Japanese popular music of the twentieth and twenty-first centuries.

Published Titles:

Supercell's *Supercell* by Keisuke Yamada

Yoko Kanno's *Cowboy Bebop Soundtrack* by Rose Bridges

Perfume's *Game* by Patrick St. Michel

Cornelius's *Fantasma* by Martin Roberts

Forthcoming Titles:

Joe Hisaishi's *My Neighbor Totoro: Soundtrack* by Kunio Hara

Nenes's *Koza Dabasa* by Henry Johnson

Shonen Knife's *Happy Hour* by Brooke McCorkle

33 1/3 Brazil

Series Editor: Jason Stanyek

Covering the genres of samba, tropicália, rock, hip hop, forró, bossa nova, heavy metal, and funk, among others, **33 1/3 Brazil** is a series devoted to in-depth examination of the most important Brazilian albums of the twentieth and twenty-first centuries.

Published Titles:

Caetano Veloso's *A Foreign Sound* by Barbara Browning

Tim Maia's *Tim Maia Racional Vols. 1 & 2* by Allen Thayer

João Gilberto and Stan Getz's *Getz/Gilberto* by Brian McCann

Dona Ivone Lara's *Sorriso Negro* by Mila Burns

Forthcoming Titles:

Gilberto Gil's *Refazenda* by Marc A. Hertzman

Milton Nascimento and Lô Borges's *The Corner Club*
    by Jonathon Grasse

Racionais MCs' *Sobrevivendo no Inferno* by Marília Gessa
    and Derek Pardue

Jorge Ben Jor's *África Brasil* by Frederick J. Moehn

Naná Vasconcelos's *Saudades* by Daniel B. Sharp

33 1/3 Europe

Series Editor: Fabian Holt

Spanning a range of artists and genres, **33 1/3 Europe** offers engaging accounts of popular and culturally significant albums of Continental Europe and the North Atlantic from the 20th and 21st centuries.

Forthcoming Titles:

Modeselektor's *Happy Birthday* by Sean Nye

Heiner Müller and Heiner Goebbels's *Wolokolamsker Chaussee*
    by Philip V. Bohlman

Ivo Papasov's *Balkanology* by Carol Silverman

Darkthrone's *A Blaze in the Northern Sky* by Ross Hagen

Dona Ivone Lara's Sorriso Negro

Mila Burns

Series Editor: Jason Stanyek

BLOOMSBURY ACADEMIC

NEW YORK · LONDON · OXFORD · NEW DELHI · SYDNEY

BLOOMSBURY ACADEMIC
Bloomsbury Publishing Inc
1385 Broadway, New York, NY 10018, USA
50 Bedford Square, London, WC1B 3DP, UK

BLOOMSBURY, BLOOMSBURY ACADEMIC and the Diana logo are
trademarks of Bloomsbury Publishing Plc

First published in the United States of America 2019

A catalog record for this book is available from the Library of Congress.

ISBN: HB: 978-1-5013-2448-2
PB: 978-1-5013-2449-9
ePDF: 978-1-5013-2450-5
eBook: 978-1-5013-2451-2

Series: $33\frac{1}{3}$ Brazil

Typeset by Deanta Global Publishing Services, Chennai
Printed and bound in the United States of America

To find out more about our authors and books visit www.bloomsbury.com
and sign up for our newsletters.

Contents

Contents

Acknowledgments

I am deeply grateful to Jason Stanyek for the invitation to write about one of my favorite albums. His sensitivity and his knowledge of Brazilian music made this adventure more challenging and pleasant. Thanks to the anonymous readers of the proposal and to all the Bloomsbury Academic team. Special thanks to Leah Babb-Rosenfeld and Rennie Alphonsa.

I am also thankful to Gilberto Velho, who helped me see beyond Dona Ivone Lara's sambas, almost two decades ago. Thanks to the Department of Latin American and Latino Studies at Lehman College, where I found a warm and welcoming intellectual environment in David Badillo, Laird Bergad, Forrest Colburn, Alyshia Galvez, Teresita Levy, Veronica Mason, Sarah Ohmer, Milagros Ricourt, and Xavier Totti. I am also grateful to Rima Brusi, José Luis Cruz, Melissa Kirk, James Mahon, Eileen Markey, Mary Phillips, Yini Rodríguez, and Orquidia Rosado Acevedo. This book is the result of my passion for Dona Ivone Lara's music and for the deeply engaging debates it provokes. I have relied on inspiring conversations with friends and mentors, including Catalina Arango, Gordon Barnes, Herman Bennett, Fatima Borba, Jonathan C. Brown, Lorena Calábria, Lawrence Cappello, Adriana Carranca, Celso Castro, Rafael Cesar, Amy Chazkel, James N. Green, Rachel Grace Newman, Marianne Gonzalez Le Saux, Jonathan Hill, Thomas Kessner, Amanda Marin, Karen Okigbo, Gabrielle Oliveira, Sandra Paine, Francisco Quinteiro Pires, Mary J. Roldán, Helena Rosenblatt, João Luiz Sampaio, and Victoria Stone-Cadena.

Paula Abreu, João Cavalcanti, Renata Chiara, Nayla Duarte, Otair Fernandes de Oliveira, Mariana Gross, Flávia Jácomo, Manu Santos, and Rogéria Vianna helped me with their time, contacts, and support. Adelzon Alves, Elifas Andreato, Adilson Barbado, Hermínio Bello de Carvalho, Leci Brandão, Nilze Carvalho, Zélia Duncan, Elisa Lucinda, Áurea Martins, Wanderson Martins, Mart'nália, Bertha Nutels, Eber Pinheiro, Bira Presidente, Juliana Ribeiro, and Zé Luiz do Império Serrano—thank you so much for your time and generosity. Pretinho da Serrinha and Leandro Braga, two of the most talented composers of Brazil, found time to listen to all of Lara's albums again to help me with the musical analysis of *Sorriso Negro*. Zé Luis Oliveira listened to each track of *Sorriso Negro* by my side, explaining all the sounds we heard. I am filled with gratitude.

I am thankful to researcher Dayene Beatriz and to the staff of the Museu da Imagem e do Som and the New York Public Library, especially the New York Public Library for the Performing Arts and Schomburg Center for Research in Black Culture. Beatriz Von Zuben, at Warner Music Brazil, helped me find information about *Sorriso Negro*.

Finally, I am grateful to my parents and my sister, with whom I heard so many of these sambas for the first time. To my husband Francisco, with whom I share a deep love for samba, books, food, and Matias. Raising Matias by his side is living proof of how much Lara's legacy matters. Not only because it makes him dance beautifully, but because it reminds us every day of the joys of living in a world where women and men share joys and responsibilities. This book is for Matias.

Introduction

Historians are used to waiting. It can take years, sometimes generations, to begin to grasp a historical event. Journalists, on the other hand, are trained to rush. In seconds, a scoop can slip through the fingers and become someone else's. As both a historian and a journalist myself, I have cherished Dona Ivone Lara's *Sorriso Negro* since hearing it for the first time. There is an urgency in its thirty-eight minutes, one that travels through centuries of Brazilian history embodying religions, Africa, women's struggles, political injustices, racism, love, samba, MPB (Brazilian Popular Music), traditions, and innovations. The album is a primary source for understanding Brazil's tense relations with race, gender, and democracy. It is also a summary of the history of Brazilian music, and a testament to Dona Ivone Lara's life and legacy.

With songs about freedom, black pride, and women's empowerment, *Sorriso Negro* reflected the fundamental changes engulfing Brazil in the final years of the military dictatorship. In February 1981, when the album was first released, the promise of a slow and gradual *Abertura* was starting to become a reality in Brazil. The "opening," after almost two decades of a violent regime, began with the signing of the Amnesty Law, in December 1979, which allowed all exiled Brazilians to return home while also protecting torturers and human rights violators from prosecution—the legislation stated the amnesty was "broad, general and unrestricted."[1] In December of that same year, the *New York Times* wrote, the "general loosens the reins in Brazil,"[2] referring to João Baptista Figueiredo, the last of the military rulers. A former cavalry officer who reportedly stated he preferred the smell of horses to the scent of the people, he was the fifth in a series of military presidents in Brazil since the 1964 coup d'état.

Sorriso Negro is the result of this political climate. It was influenced by the challenges of women and blacks in Brazil and, at the same time, it shaped the fight for equality. Besides being a symbol of movements for gender and racial equality in the country, the album also speaks to Lara's lifetime. For more than ninety years, she was constantly confronted with difficulties. As a black woman who chose to be a samba composer, Dona Ivone Lara had to fight society's expectations and prejudices her entire life.

Violent oppression of civil liberties was the norm during the dictatorship.[3] In the early 1980s, the sense of an imminent return to democracy allowed the feminist movement that had emerged in the late 1960s to develop fully. Until the late 1970s, women's political activism was timidly connected with the suggestion of a revision of gender roles that consigned them to a secondary place in Brazilian society. The primary focus, for men and women, was to fight the authoritarian regime. With the weakening of the imposed government, the question of women's political participation and rights became a central concern. The issue at stake was not only how to put an end to the dictatorship, but what role specific underrepresented groups would play in a civil society from which they had long been disenfranchised.

The creation of two magazines dedicated to the fight for equal rights for women, *Brasil Mulher* and *Nós Mulheres*, and the publication of the book *Memórias das Mulheres do Exílio*, in 1980, reflect the climate of change in place when Lara released *Sorriso Negro*.[4] The early 1980s also brought to fruition a dramatic increase in the participation of women in the workforce and the political realm. Before the coup d'état of 1964, only 0.6 percent of Brazilian legislators were women. In the first democratic elections after the dictatorship, in 1985, the number increased to almost 6 percent, and included the emergence, as a politician, of Benedita da Silva, a black woman from a slum in Rio de Janeiro.[5] However, the persistence of old assumptions accompanied this process: women were still responsible for taking care of domestic work, raising children, and settling for typically "female jobs." Samba composers were (and still are) predominantly male.

The album also questioned the position of blacks in Brazilian society. The title and many of the songs establish racial injustice as a central theme. It was not by accident. In the early 1980s, when *Sorriso Negro* was released, the Black Movement gained strength in the country. In a process similar to the shift in gender debates, the topic of race surfaced much more aggressively after the *Abertura*. During the dictatorship, the government embraced the anti-racialist narrative in an attempt to silence the Black Movement. Its militants were deemed unpatriotic for mimicking the US Civil Rights Movement. With the military regime tarnished, however, black groups demanded protections and changes in the legislation. One of their most significant victories was the establishment, in the constitution of 1988, of racial discrimination as a crime subject to imprisonment without bail.[6]

The torture and killing of Robson Silveira da Luz, whom the police accused of stealing fruits from a street market, and episodes of racial discrimination in institutions such as the Clube de Regatas Tietê were tipping points that culminated in the growth of the Black Movement in Brazil. The Movimento Negro Unificado, founded in July 1978 with the purpose of reacting to "racial violence," is one example.[7] The group embodied ideals associated with national heroes, such as Zumbi dos Palmares, as well as those associated with foreign champions of the fight for civil rights, such as Malcolm X.[8] Among Afro-Brazilians, "black is beautiful" became a chant stronger than "democracy now." The culmination also reflected a revision of race relations across Brazilian society. The racial gap in the job market, the absence of black representatives in political positions, and the deep economic crisis were now addressed by a black intellectual elite who refused to accept discourses of "tolerance."[9]

Zé Luiz do Império Serrano, former president of the *Velha Guarda* of the samba school that he adopted as his stage name, remembers that the release of *Sorriso Negro* was a seminal moment for the Black Movement and for samba in general. It arrived at a time when the repression of the 1960s and 1970s was fading.

> It was a fertile moment for samba in Rio de Janeiro and pagode in São Paulo. In the early 1980s, groups such as Fundo de Quintal and singers like Zeca Pagodinho, Roberto Ribeiro, Clara Nunes, and Beth Carvalho reached large audiences. The album had a tremendous impact because she was the first black woman to occupy a prominent position as a songwriter.[10]

The seminal works of Abdias do Nascimento and Edison Carneiro, published decades earlier, gained visibility in Brazilian public life;[11] Gilberto Freyre, Caio Prado Junior, and Florestan Fernandes were now at the center of a broad debate on historical racial inequality.[12] Empowered black activists, artists, and intellectuals saw in the return to democracy an opportunity to question dominant racial ideologies. The idea that Brazil was a nation free of prejudices, propagated since the nineteenth century, was now described as a "myth." The quest for affirmative action was at the heart of Brazilian society. Although this book focuses on *Sorriso Negro* and is far from being a study of the Black Movement in Brazil, it positions Dona Ivone Lara's album as a symbol of the flourishing of gender and racial activism in proto-democratic Brazil. The above cited authors were central to shaping the theoretical framework this book relies on to understand the context of *Sorriso Negro*'s release. The analysis of the "racialization" of Lara's music in connection with this new political consciousness in the late 1970s and early 1980s also relates to the work of scholars who accompanied the shift in the debates of race in the country in the 1970s and 1980s.[13]

This book is divided into three parts. In the first one, I dissect songs that are associated to the questioning of gender inequality in Brazil. I analyze "A Sereia Guiomar" (The Mermaid Guiomar), "Alguém Me Avisou" (Someone Told Me), "De Braços Com a Felicidade" (Arm in Arm with Happiness), "Meu Fim de Carnaval Não Foi Ruim" (The End of My Carnival Was Not Bad), and "Nunca Mais" (Never Again) not only from a musical perspective but also from a historical one, in the context of the rise of feminism in the late 1970s Brazil. I also discuss the presence of Maria Bethânia and Rosinha de Valença in *Sorriso Negro*, Lara's biography, and the region of Serrinha, in Rio de Janeiro, where she flourished as a composer. Part 2 evokes the partnerships Lara did with several musicians. With "Os Cinco Bailes da História do Rio" (The Five Balls of the History of Rio de Janeiro) and "Adeus de um Poeta" (Farewell to a Poet) I look at her partnership with Silas de Oliveira; "Me Deixa Ficar" (Let Me Stay) is the starting point to talk about Delcio Carvalho, and "Unhas" (Nails), Hermínio Bello de Carvalho. Lara wrote "Tendência" (Tendency) with Jorge Aragão, a leading figure in the early years of the *pagode* trend. I also discuss the emergence of this movement during the dictatorship in Brazil, as well as bossa nova and Black Rio. The album cover is also explained in the words of its creator, Elifas Andreato, who considers it to be a political work. The final part addresses the prominence of the debate about race in *Sorriso Negro*, with the title song and "Axé de Ianga" (Axé of Ianga). I discuss the duet with Jorge Ben in "Sorriso Negro" (Black Smile), his importance to a new perspective of Afro-Brazilian music, the inspirations for the two tracks, and what they ended up inspiring in the Brazilian Black Movement.

Dona Ivone Lara was never an activist for social and political change, in the strict definition of the term.[14] She did not act directly and openly with the intent of promoting racial and gender equality. She rarely joined demonstrations and never identified herself as politically engaged. While the black power movement gained prominence around the world in the 1960s and 1970s, she embraced the idea of resisting the arrival of soul music, claiming that samba was the real representation of what it was to be a Brazilian.[15] She sang with Clementina de Jesus—also a samba icon who only became renowned in her later years—and Candeia on a now-classic rendition of "Sou Mais o Samba," which states, *"Eu não sou africano nem norte-americano . . . Sou mais o samba brasileiro"* (I am not African or North American . . . I prefer the Brazilian samba).[16]

Although several musicians and samba composers refused to discuss discrimination during the dictatorship, echoing the racial-harmony narrative of the regime, *Sorriso Negro* reflects a different moment: one of openness and courage.[17] Lara decided that the title of the album would be "Black Smile" because it was a call for equal opportunities. Curiously enough, the title song is one of only two on the album that Dona Ivone Lara did not write. (The other was "Adeus de um Poeta," an homage to her deceased partner Silas de Oliveira.) Despite valuing her work as a composer more than her singing, she chose someone else's song as the title because she thought it epitomized the message the album conveyed. The cover is a declaration of black pride: a close-up portrayal of Dona Ivone Lara, her dark skin, bare shoulders, and red lips highlighted by the artwork of Elifas Andreato. She wears three beaded necklaces, a reminder of African culture in Brazil. "A Sereia Guiomar," the song that opens the album, is often interpreted to be about female strength, and "Alguém me Avisou" is usually thought to be about female strategies to achieve respect in male-dominated environments. Rosinha de Valença, a renowned guitar player and composer and close friend of Dona Ivone Lara, was responsible for the musical arrangements of the album.[18]

Brazilian singer and historian Juliana Ribeiro considers Lara's strategy to be one of the most potent forms of activism. She claims that Lara's empowering of black women does not come from acts, but from poise and trajectory.[19]

> In the case of Clementina de Jesus, we are talking about a black woman who worked as a domestic servant her entire life and, as an elderly person, decided to be on a stage and perform songs related to her own experience. Lara manages to do the same for a longer period and as part of the mainstream music in Brazil. She presented herself as an artist directly connected to the music industry, which I don't see as a problem per se, but as an opportunity to make herself renowned for a longer time.[20]

That Lara was a black woman, writing and singing songs about race and gender, makes the songs of *Sorriso Negro* a powerful act of resistance. "Each one has a different manner of doing things, but there is no denying that she was a pathbreaker. Showing her songs in public, writing a *samba-enredo* at a time when women didn't have any space in the samba universe, are forms of engagement," says singer and songwriter Nilze Carvalho.[21]

One cannot consider the album, however, to be a typical example of activism in itself. It is a materialization of what I call *resistance by existence*. I use Michel Foucault's definition of resistance—not as antagonism or political agitation, but as a broad opposition to power—which embodies diverse possibilities of political action.[22] I also borrow from James C. Scott's concept of hidden transcripts, a kind of secret code that underrepresented groups create to criticize and question the powerful behind their backs.[23] *Resistance by existence* is not merely an oppositional act, but the combination of a highly conscious existence with a tremendous impact on power relations, reshaping intersubjective understanding and transforming society.[24] Lara developed a sensible strategy to overcome the challenges of a black woman in twentieth-century Brazil, one that served as an example for the following generations. Her strong presence on stage, her famous countermelodies—which resemble traditional sub-Saharan African chants—and her biography embody, in several ways, the resilience of Brazilian black women in the face of substantial challenges.

I have talked to Dona Ivone Lara several times, on many occasions, for my previous book, which studied her pathbreaking career.[25] One thread that ran through all these conversations was a narrative of intention. "I did it because I wanted to," she would state regarding her professional choices, her family, and many other aspects of her life. Her individual and independent decisions, dissonant with the society and the times in which she came of age and built her career, were part of a negotiation, a strategy to achieve a higher goal. One example is that, for years, she did not acknowledge in public that she was the composer of her songs. Instead, she let her cousin Mestre Fuleiro, who was a songwriter for the samba school Império Serrano, introduce the songs as if he had written them. Lara affirmed she was not angry about that, but rather happy to see that her work was good.[26] Composer and pianist Leandro Braga states that "samba grows within a culture of survival, which often includes, until nowadays, subservience."[27] From an early age, Lara demonstrated a high level of *attention a la vie*, from which she developed her own form of activism, one without open political engagement.[28]

Hermínio Bello de Carvalho, the cocomposer of "Unhas," the fourth track of *Sorriso Negro*, contends that there is no way of looking at the album without thinking of its political connotations.[29] He claims that it is an act of political activism to bring to mainstream media someone who is "marginalized in the process" of democratization, who is not part of the perceived reality of success as portrayed by Brazilian television and movies of the time. "Clementina de Jesus, Jovelina Pérola Negra, and Dona Ivone Lara are, even if indirectly, making a political statement when they take the stage, sing, and offer their essence to the audience."[30] Singer Mart'nália goes beyond this, stating that Lara's songs and life were a form of including black women in the national narrative.

> The way she dances, her posture, the fact that she is a woman in a masculine world, all that opened the possibility for women to be part of the samba universe—not only cooking or as backing vocalists, *cabrochas*, always assisting. She made it clear that the same woman who serves is the woman who writes songs, melodies, and gives strength not only to other women but to the entire samba environment.[31]

Radio personality Adelzon Alves produced Lara's first two solo albums and the compilation records she participated in before that. Lara sings "Tiê" and "Agradeço a Deus" ("I Thank God") on *Quem samba fica? Fica! Volume 2* (The ones who dance the samba stay? They do! Volume 2), released in 1974. In the album, Alves introduces her as a pathbreaking woman and acknowledges that it is revolutionary to have her in that group: "Ivone Lara, besides being an excellent mother, housewife, nurse, and social assistant is a great songwriter, plays the *cavaquinho* in a way no *malandro*[32] can complain of and is a member of the wing of the *Baianas* of Império Serrano samba school." He also describes the album's cover picture, in which Lara is playing at a *roda de samba*[33] at Castelo Branco, "a men-only club, at Edgar Romero Street, close to Serrinha, that, for her, her *cavaquinho*, and her melodies, always makes an exception [*and opens its doors*]."[34]

Born in Botafogo and raised in the northern area of Rio de Janeiro, Dona Ivone Lara moved between many different universes during her almost one century of life. She was born Yvonne, with a "Y" and double "N," on April 13, 1921. Samba was in her blood. Her mother, Emerentina da Silva, was a singer in *ranchos*, traditional samba groups that paraded in the streets of Rio de Janeiro in the early twentieth century.[35] Her father, João Lara, played seven-string guitar in the same groups. They met and fell in love during a carnival parade. Tragedy marked her humble childhood. Her father was hit by a car and died when she was two years old. Her mother remarried a year later to a "very good man," according to Lara.[36] Venino José da Silva took care of Emerentina's two daughters, Yvonne and Elza, and they had three other kids together. Emerentina died when Lara was a teenager. At the time, Lara lived in the boarding school Colégio Municipal Orsina da Fonseca. Among her teachers were Lucília Villa-Lobos, wife of the composer Heitor Villa-Lobos, and Zaíra de Oliveira, a famous black singer who had won the Escola de Música do Rio de Janeiro contest in 1921. With them, Lara learned music, developed a talent for composition, and understood the challenges that being a woman imposed on songwriters.[37]

Besides her teachers and her cousin, Mestre Fuleiro, a few other people were instrumental in her musical development.

At twenty-six, she married Oscar Costa, son of Alfredo Costa, the founder of the samba school Prazer da Serrinha. It was Oscar who invited his friend, the influential composer and *sambista*, Silas de Oliveira, to join the school. In 1965, Dona Ivone Lara coauthored with Oliveira and Bacalhau the composition "Os Cinco Bailes da História do Rio," the first official *samba-enredo* written by a woman.[38] She also became the first woman to be part of an *ala dos compositores*, the group of composers that writes *sambas-enredo*. A beautiful and slower version of the song appears on *Sorriso Negro*. It sounds like a resistance to the changes *sambas-enredo* had gone through during the 1970s.[39]

Pretinho da Serrinha has played with Lara several times, since a very early age. Today, he is one of the most celebrated songwriters and musicians of Império Serrano's new generation of *sambistas*. He says she has never been one to pick a fight or make political statements, but her success at a time when women faced many limitations opened an avenue of possibilities to younger musicians: "She was a leader, a pioneer. She was the first woman to write a *samba-enredo*. 'Os Cinco Bailes da História do Rio' was not the champion of that carnival parade. It lost but it is still far better known than the one that won. Her existence changed everything for us. Look at the number of people who have her as a central reference. Samba's history can be divided into two periods: before and after Dona Ivone Lara."[40]

Atlantic/WEA released *Sorriso Negro* on February 26, 1981. However, the real launch of the album happened a few months later, in a limited engagement at Teatro Ipanema. José Ramos Tinhorão, now known as one of the most prolific researchers of Brazilian music, wrote a review of the album for *Jornal do Brasil*. He stated that it was the confirming proof of her quality, one that "was above all the others, including that of an excellent creator of melodic lines: D. Ivone [*Lara*] has one of the most seductive and hot black voices of Brazilian popular music."[41] Other critics, however, had a few sour words about the live performance. Not regarding Lara, whom they described as a great "singer, composer, interpreter of a perfect repertoire in its genre, one that is not only traditional, but alive and intense."[42] They complained about the musicians. Helviu Vilela (piano), Jorginho Degos (bass), Papão (drums), and Helcio Milito (percussion) "insist on accompanying the traditional style of the star with bossa nova beats and swings. Individually, all of the musicians are great. But together, they create a *pororoca*," the critics wrote, referring to the Amazonian tidal bore resulting from the encounter of two rivers that do not mix.[43] In the indigenous language Tupi, *pororoca* can be translated as "great roar." Helviu Vilela was a celebrated jazz and bossa nova musician, and Helcio Milito was one of the members of Tamba Trio, an emblematic bossa nova group. The only three musicians absolved of the criticism were Sereno do Cacique (tantan), Bira Presidente (pandeiro), and Ubirany (repenique), cofounders of Fundo de Quintal, one of the most traditional samba groups in the country.[44]

The tension between bossa nova and samba, traditional and commercial music, was also at the center of the album. The lack of documents about it makes it hard to say precisely how many copies were sold and what was the major audience, but in Warner Music's full product report the "major genre" is samba and the "minor genre" field is left blank.[45] There are no references to the musicians who recorded in *Sorriso Negro*. It was Lara's third solo album and the first one produced by Sérgio Cabral, a renowned journalist, producer, and researcher, who authored more than a dozen books about samba. He brought a slower pace to some already famous songs and a more MPB (Brazilian Popular Music) style, with Maria Bethânia and Jorge Ben as special guests—a very different lineup from Mestre Alcídes, Manacéa, and other historical samba figures who were present in the first two records, produced by Adelzon Alves.

Brazilian singer Zélia Duncan, who recorded several of Lara's songs and wrote the description of her pictures for the book *Álbum de Retratos*, defines *Sorriso Negro* as a watershed. While some claim that Cabral brought a commercial tone to the album, while Alves kept samba's traditional roots, she states that the final impact is what matters. "An album with songs such as 'Sereia Guiomar,' 'Alguém Me Avisou,' and 'Tendência,' is destined to be a classic."[46] *Sorriso Negro* did more than merely connect Dona Ivone Lara to broader audiences. The album is a symbol of her talent, with songs that have found a place in the canonical repertoire of samba. With this work, she became widely recognized as a central figure in Brazilian culture, but her path was not an easy one. As she claims in "Alguém Me Avisou," one of the album's most famous songs, she was warned by someone to "*pisar este chão devagarinho*," which can be translated idiomatically into English as "watch your step" or "tread lightly in this area."

Sorriso Negro has twelve tracks, five of which Lara composed alone, five of which she coauthored, and two which were written by others. The album also marks the solidification of her lifelong partnership with Delcio Carvalho, coauthor of two songs on *Sorriso Negro* and dozens more in her career. An interesting aspect of this partnership is that Lara usually wrote the music, at a time when it was perceived as the more masculine aspect of songwriting, and Carvalho wrote the lyrics. Lara met him through her husband, Oscar. She defined their alliance as "a genuine appreciation for one another. We would sit, talk. It never happened that I wasn't sure about a lyric he wrote or thought it was different from what I expected. I always loved his songs."[47]

The meetings with Delcio Carvalho and other collaborators only took place during the weekends and holidays. On weekdays, she had a full-time job as a nurse and social assistant. Even when introducing herself to admirers, she used to say, "Nice to meet you. I am Ivone Lara, a social assistant." In her youth, seeking stability, she applied to the traditional Nursing School Alfredo Pinto, in Rio de Janeiro: "Many people in the samba universe were employed in hospitals. I have worked with a bunch of them. For instance, the mother of Paulinho da Viola, wife of Mr. Paulo Faria, who was already a very renowned musician, was also a nurse. He was a musician, but relied on her regular job."[48]

Working as a social assistant, Dona Ivone Lara was also a close witness to crucial moments in Brazilian history. She was an assistant to Dr. Nise da Silveira, a pioneer in using music and the arts to treat patients with mental health issues.[49] Only after retirement, when she was fifty-six years old, did Lara feel she could finally dedicate herself exclusively to her musical career. She released *Sorriso Negro* during this period. At this point, samba was not a persecuted rhythm but a national symbol, incorporated into the collective imagination and appropriated by the dictatorship as the most Brazilian of Brazilian art forms.[50]

Pretinho da Serrinha sees a progression from the first LP to *Sorriso Negro*. *Samba, Minha Verdade, Samba, Minha Raiz* (Samba, My Truth, Samba, My Roots), he says, is a more traditional album, with arrangements and recording quality that allow for one to listen to the noises and murmurs of the instruments. *Sorriso de Criança* (Child's Smile) has a different sonority and includes wind instruments that are not typical in a *roda de samba*. *Sorriso Negro* is much sharper and embraces a multitude of instruments.

> The melodic line is always following her style. There is no way one can listen to a song she wrote and not notice her authorship. There is a romanticism, a lyricism. . . . She is a bit classical, too, and touches the listener deep in the heart. If you listen to her with your eyes closed, you will certainly cry.[51]

For Eber Pinheiro, music producer and mixer, *Sorriso Negro* belongs to a select list of avant-garde albums that will never get old. "There is nothing that tells you it is a 1980s album. When you listen to it, the feeling is that it could have been recorded at any time. But only in Brazil."[52] Composer and pianist Leandro Braga, who transcribed thirteen of Lara's compositions for the songbook *Primeira Dama* (First Lady), states that it is all about lyricism. "That is what characterizes the melodies of Dona Ivone Lara. Many long notes and sudden jumps that make a perfect contrast while also complementing the rhythmic base. I have heard it being attributed to a choral experience, but I cannot attest to that. I think one can almost call it a 'mother's samba.'"[53]

Lara's talent and originality were recognized late in her life, after she retired from her full-time job as a social assistant. She then toured Europe, Africa, and the Americas. In 2002, she received the Prêmio Caras de Música in the category Best Samba Album, with *Nasci para Sonhar e Cantar* (I Was Born to Dream and to Sing). In 2010, she was the honoree at the *Prêmio da Música Brasileira* (Brazilian Music Award). Two years later, in what she considers one of the highest honors of her career, Lara's life was the theme of the samba school Império Serrano for the 2012 carnival parade. In May 2015, she was the subject of an art exhibition at Itaú Cultural, in São Paulo. While I was writing this book, Lara performed in several concerts, not with the vigor of the early years, but sitting in a chair and singing with passion each one of her fabulous melodies—and still with her typical combination of power and tenderness. She died on April 16, 2018, of cardiorespiratory failure, at the age of ninety-six.[54] She left not only an incontestable musical legacy but also one of fight for equality which continues to inspire generations in Brazil.

Part 1

Women and samba

If art is a mirror of society, then we can see from the roles women play in the samba environment that much has changed in Brazil, but there is still a long way to go. From the birth of the rhythm through its evolution into a national symbol, the vast majority of samba composers and instrumentalists were men. One of them, Moacyr Luz, suggested an explanation. A renowned musician who has had more than one hundred of his songs recorded by some of the most famous Brazilian artists, such as Maria Bethânia, Gilberto Gil, Beth Carvalho, and Zeca Pagodinho, Luz once told me that "women don't write sambas because they don't go to bars."[1] Men create songs over beers and peanuts, and Brazilian society just does not allow women to be part of such an environment. They can be singers, muses, or both, but creating melodies and writing lyrics are usually reserved for men. Carmen Miranda, Elis Regina, Araci de Almeida, Clara Nunes, Linda Batista, Clementina de Jesus, Beth Carvalho, Alcione, and many other musical artists have included samba in their repertoires. Very few of these women, however, have been giving voice to their own compositions.

Another conventional role for women in the samba scene is the important figure of the *tias* (aunties, in English).[2] An auntie is not a muse or a singer, but a kind of counselor. Hilária Batista de Almeida—better known as Tia Ciata—is the most renowned of them. She was a cook from Bahia who moved to the neighborhood of Praça Onze in Rio de Janeiro in the 1870s.[3] João do Rio, a homosexual journalist of African descent who chronicled Rio de Janeiro's poor areas in the early twentieth century, called her "a black of low character, vulgar, and presumptuous."[4] He described her role in Candomblé— which combines Roman Catholic, African, and indigenous Brazilian components—with contempt and fear: "The people of her town say that she has driven a distinguished lady crazy, by giving her a mix for a certain disease of the uterus."[5]

The area of Praça Onze was celebrated as "Little Africa," and Ciata made daily efforts to keep it worthy of the nickname. She hosted events such as Candomblé rituals, and parties wherein groups of musicians came together to experiment, improvise, and taste African food. Artists and composers came from far and wide to introduce their most recent creations. Her house became the mecca of African culture in the then capital of Brazil and is now considered one of the birthplaces of samba. "Pelo Telefone" (By Phone), deemed to be the first song of the genre, was composed there in 1916. There were other prominent female figures in the area at the time, but it is Ciata who is remembered today as the godmother of samba. Lira Neto states that, actually,

> just like many other black women [who were] treated with reverence as *tias* by the community—Tia Bebiana, Tia Celeste, Tia Dadá, Tia Davina, Tia Gracinda, Tia Mônica, Tia Perpétua, Tia Perciliana, Tia Sadata, and Tia Veridiana—Ciata had a leading role in the community and an unquestionable leadership in the daily lives of all residents of the neighborhoods of Saúde, Cidade Nova, and Gamboa.[6]

Even today, samba schools pay homage to Tia Ciata in the *ala das baianas*, which is mandatory in all parades.[7] Dona Ivone Lara was a member of this wing from a young age. In the show to launch *Sorriso Negro*, she wore a beautiful, heavy dress that was typical of a *baiana*. The critics acknowledged the power of such a tradition, stating that it created an impact when she entered the stage. However, they complained it was "beautiful for a carnival parade, but ruined Lara's dance."[8] There are still many *tias* in samba schools today. They are most often elderly women who have dedicated many years to the school and now enjoy some influence, but not necessarily great authority. The honorary title confers respect but no formal decision-making powers.[9]

It was—and still is—in the houses of the *tias* that the samba community got together for endless *rodas de samba*. Just as in the time of Tia Ciata, during Lara's active professional years composers continued to use these occasions to showcase their new songs, or even to write *in-loco* pieces that would later become hits in the samba world. The mouthwatering smell of *feijoada*, the cold beer, and the simple tables around the backyard formed the perfect setting for powerful networks of socialization.[10] In post-slavery Brazil, the dynamics of the traditional *bourgeois* family did not apply to most of the African and Afro-Brazilian families. Not only were women in charge of raising kids and working inside the house but they also had to join the labor market, frequently in informal jobs. Tia Ciata was one of many women from Bahia who brought to Rio de Janeiro the tradition of forming groups of organized workers in small and casual business such as food trade, sewing services, and rental of carnival clothes. Mônica

Pimenta Velloso explains that this experience in the job market "influenced the personality of these women, changing the way they thought, felt, and integrated with reality. In contrast with women from other social segments, they behaved uninhibited and had a looser language and greater freedom of locomotion and initiative."[11]

The *tias* were the hosts and bosses of their houses. They were the rulers of the place where sambas were created, cocomposers met, and decisions about the future of samba schools were made. Women, therefore, have been a crucial part of the history of samba since its very early days, but only as community organizers, performers, or simply as inspiration for male songwriters. Dona Ivone Lara, however, was not a *tia*, a singer, or a muse. She wrote songs and sang them. It is difficult to find an appropriate title for her, which in itself demonstrates how peculiarly male chauvinist the samba environment is. Lara became known as the "first-lady of samba," *primeira-dama*, a title that completely contradicts her pioneering work and her independence as a composer, since it implies the presence of a strong man beside her, a male "head of state."

A Sereia Guiomar

Half-woman, half-fish, a mermaid (*sereia*, in Portuguese) is a mythical creature that appears in the popular culture all over the world. They are frequently perceived as treacherous beings who can seduce and destroy. In Brazilian folklore, the most famous of these mighty creatures is Iara, which means "lady of the water" in Tupi.[12] Iara has another characteristic that is somehow indicative of the Brazilian societal expectations for women: she sings. Her irresistible voice attracts men to the bottom of the river, draws them to their certain death. The few who can survive her approach end up mad, destroyed by her enchantments. Lara's decision to open the album with "A Sereia Guiomar" (The Mermaid Guiomar) is deeply related to her admiration of a strong Brazilian woman, Maria Bethânia. They became good friends in 1978, when Bethânia recorded Lara's "Sonho Meu" (My Dream) with another symbol of *baianidade*, Gal Costa. The tune became a hit and helped Bethânia's album *Álibi* sell more than a million copies, a first for a woman in the country. It also turned Lara into a celebrity even beyond the samba environment.

It all started with a mutual friend, guitar player and composer Rosinha de Valença, who introduced Maria Bethânia to the song "Sonho Meu." A few years later, Lara's friendship with Valença would produce more fruits. Valença made the musical arrangements for most of the songs of *Sorriso Negro* and was the conductor for several of them. Her influence can be heard throughout the album. Born in the city of Valença, in the state of Rio de Janeiro, the acoustic guitar player was a prodigy. She was only 12 years old when she began to play in local events. Ten years later, Valença moved to the city of Rio de Janeiro and very soon became a fixture in the legendary Beco das Garrafas, an area full or nightclubs where the most famous musicians in the country performed. There, she met musical producer Aloysio de Oliveira, the director of record label Elenco.[13]

Oliveira was so astonished by Valença's talent that he not only invited her to record her first album, *Apresentando Rosinha de Valença* (Introducing Rosinha de Valença), but also asked her to produce it. It was 1964, and she became respected in a male-dominated environment. Being a woman intensively influenced her playing. In an interview in 1972, she said:

> I was a woman who needed luck because I was the only one dealing with a huge number of male acoustic guitar players, a bunch of men who were not about to give me a place. I almost had to pull the strings off the guitar so people would understand that I could play. I don't know how many times did I purposefully play the chords very strongly to wake people up, so they would shut up a little and pay attention: when an artist plays he has to be heard. It does not matter if you're wearing a skirt or a brief.[14]

Valença and Lara had experienced similar challenges in life, and they connected immediately. In *Sorriso Negro,* it is clear that they communicated musically as well.

Zé Luis Oliveira, a Brazilian composer, saxophonist, flutist, producer, and arranger, was very active in the early 1980s, having recorded and performed with Caetano Veloso, Gilberto Gil, Gal Costa, and Cazuza. He also played with Rosinha de Valença and thinks her arrangements and conducting are key to threading songs in *Sorriso Negro.* "There are instruments not very typical of samba at that time, and also the melodic patterns, the voicings, and the harmony are all very sophisticated."[15] "A Sereia Guiomar" begins with an instrumental introduction that evokes the smell of salted water. The nautical atmosphere is the result of an affectionate conversation among flutes, a *balafon* (an African marimba), and a soprano saxophone. Just like the dialogue between Valença and Lara, this is a conversation between traditional samba and the new Brazilian popular music. "It also carries the duality of the 2/4 and the 6/8, which is a very African element," explains Oliveira.

An ensemble of female voices sings the chorus "*A Sereia Guiomar mora em alto mar*" (The Mermaid Guiomar lives on the high seas), with Maria Bethânia's voice a little louder than the others. Then Dona Ivone Lara sings alone "*Como é bonito meu Deus*" (How beautiful is it, my God), and the choir completes the verse "*a lenda desta sereia*" (The legend of this mermaid). It is an inspired flirtation with Bahia's *samba de roda*[16] and Rio de Janeiro's *partido-alto*, in which the main vocalist invites the audience to sing along, in a kind of call-and-answer pattern. In this duet, Bethânia and Lara take turns singing.[17] The *surdo*—a large bass drum used in Brazilian music—keeps the *partido-alto* pattern throughout the song, while flute and soprano saxophone take turns counterpointing with the vocals, courting the Brazilian rhythms of *choro* and *gafieira*.[18]

Samba's most basic rhythm has two beats, with four strokes each, in a 2/4 time structure. What gives it a unique swing is the syncopation, which means that the strong beat is suspended and the weak accentuated. Author Barbara Browning has described samba's syncopation as the body saying what cannot be spoken: "This suspension leaves the body with a hunger that can only be satisfied by filling the silence with motion. Samba, the dance, cannot exist without the suppression of a strong beat."[19] For Muniz Sodré, the prolonged sound of the weak beat over the strong beat that creates the syncopated rhythm is a form of resistance, a way of pretending submission to the European tonal system while at the same time rhythmically destabilizing it.[20] He argues that syncopation is not a Brazilian invention and was present rhythmically in African music and melodically in Portuguese music. In a controversial argument, Sodré considers that the rhythm is more prevalent than the melody in samba, which is also a way of suggesting that its African heritage takes priority over its European.[21]

The encounter between Africa and Europe is apparent in Lara's stage performances. Some consider samba to be a mix between African *lundu* and Portuguese *modinha*. Lara has a unique dance that became her trademark.[22] She pulls up her long skirt, just enough to show her feet in small steps, reminiscent of the hops in *jongo* and Candomblé circles. The *samba de roda* follows a pulse similar to the African rhythm *lundu*, but at a slower pace. Indeed, Lara's dancing style resembles the *lundu* dance, in which the performer steps firmly on the floor, adding another layer of percussion to the song.

In Dona Ivone Lara and Maria Bethânia's performance of "A Sereia Guiomar" the wind instruments in the introduction indicate that hers is not a traditional take. The arrangements are reminiscent of Bethânia's previous albums, in which several songs relied on wind instruments. The exception, then, were the songs composed by Lara, in which samba percussion instruments and electric keyboards prevail. In Bethânia's album *Álibi*, "Sonho Meu" opens with the fingerpicking of an acoustic guitar, followed by a *cuíca* and the strumming of a *cavaquinho*. It is the traditional samba, conducted by the *tamborim*.

"A Sereia Guiomar" retains one of the main characteristics of Lara's partnerships with songwriter Delcio Carvalho: the lyrics and the music intertwine and communicate as if they were in an ongoing and intense dialogue. In this case, the words refer to the Brazilian ocean, the moon, fishermen, and the legends of mermaids. It is almost an invitation to travel to Bahia. There is more to it, however. The lyrics also explain that the mermaid's voice exerts "dominance" over men. Brazilian singer Zélia Duncan, who recorded "Sereia Guiomar" in 1999 with Lara, calls the song a "strong feminine samba." She explains that it is impossible to divide the composer's work from her personal achievements.

> She has a unique role in the world of samba and therefore of Brazilian music. She has unfolded the male-dominated wilderness of samba-songwriters, and her *contracantos* (vocal counterpoints) are the most famous and beautiful ever heard. Dona Ivone Lara is Dona Ivone Lara also because she is black and brings the majesty of her color in her singing and her attitudes. Only she could have become who she became, and her existence gave strength to black Brazilian women.[23]

De Braços Com a Felicidade

Dona Ivone Lara's passion for Salvador, the first Brazilian capital and principal port for slave traffic, grew during the recording of the movie *A Força de Xangô*, directed by Iberê Cavalcanti, and released in 1977. In the film, Lara not only sings but acts in a leading role. She plays Zulmira de Yansã, the wife of the main character. Tonho Tiê (performed by Geraldo Rosa) is known as a philanderer and is a "son of Xangô" in the African-Brazilian religion of Candomblé, which suggests he will never be satisfied with only one lover.[24] They meet during carnival, and Tonho promises to be forever faithful. The years pass, they age, and he goes back to being a womanizer. Zulmira then makes a "*macumba* for Yansã," a kind of witchcraft to take revenge on her husband. Both characters are deeply rooted in the traditions of Candomblé.[25]

Besides the movie, Maria Bethânia was also an essential part of Lara's connection with Bahia. Following the success of Bethânia and Gal Costa's rendition of "Sonho Meu," Lara recorded an astonishingly beautiful version of the song with Clementina de Jesus for the album *Clementina e Convidados*. In 1980, Lara went back to Salvador to join Clementina, whom she called her *mana* (sister), in a concert at the traditional Vila Velha Theater, which the *baianos* affectionately call "the Vila." The theater is still considered to be a symbol of resistance to the dictatorship. Singer Juliana Ribeiro, who performed there in a concert featuring only songs from Clementina de Jesus's repertoire, calls it a revolutionary institution. "People from all over the country—from all over the world—come to perform here because of its history of being a black theater and a theater of resistance."[26] Having Clementina de Jesus and Dona Ivone Lara together on stage in a "black theater" known for questioning the authoritarian regime was a powerful symbol of the changes black women were going through at that moment in history. The passion for Bahia is present not only in "A Sereia Guiomar" but also in the second and third songs of the album, for which Lara composed both music and lyrics: "De Braços com a Felicidade" (Arm in Arm with Happiness)—in which Lara states that she went back to Rio de Janeiro "*Pra ver se esquecia / O amor que eu deixei lá na Bahia*" (To try to forget / The love that I left in Bahia)—and "Alguém Me Avisou" in which the author claims to be originally from Bahia.

"De Braços com a Felicidade" starts with an improvisation that sounds like a continuation of the "la la ia" (samba vocalizing) which ends "A Sereia Guiomar," as if keeping the same Bahian atmosphere, full of vitality. The seven-string acoustic guitar, the *cavaquinho* (a Brazilian small four-string guitar), and the very prominent *surdo*, however, suggest a Rio de Janeiro mood. This intertwining of Bahia and traditional Rio de Janeiro samba is a thread that runs through the album. "One example is that the *balafon* and the woodblock, instruments more connected to Bahia, frequently replace the *agogô* bells, which is a very *carioca* instrument," observes Zé Luis Oliveira.[27]

Despite these instrumental connections, "De Braços com a Felicidade" is a straight-up *carioca* samba, keeping the traditional "call and answer" verse structure. All the baselines are secured by the seven-string guitar, as usually done in traditional choro and samba. The melody gets more complex, following a meandering line that dialogues with the bold harmony and arrangements. In the end, the lyrics go back to the idea of keeping the encounter between Rio and Bahia forever in her heart. She sings that embracing happiness, she would invite nostalgia (saudade) to live with her in Rio.[28] While she repeats the word "Rio" in the fade-out, the trombones play lines typical of Rio de Janeiro tambourines.

In context, the song feels like an appropriate transition between "A Sereia Guiomar" and "Alguém Me Avisou," the three of which form the Bahian triad of the album. Pianist Leandro Braga explains that Bahia and Africa are in the roots of any samba.[29] However, the samba from Rio de Janeiro has never existed in Africa or Bahia. While the rhythmic foundations and the syncopation do come from African ancestor praise songs, samba from Bahia and Rio de Janeiro manifest differently.

> "A Sereia Guiomar" was recorded in the Ijexá rhythm, which is part of the Candomblé ritual. The mixture of black culture from Bahia with what slaves brought directly to Rio de Janeiro generated the *samba carioca*. Therefore, to say that samba was born in Bahia is only true for samba from Bahia. However, to say that Dona Ivone Lara's music has nothing to do with Bahia is also inaccurate.[30]

In this particular track, Lara's voice has a brighter tone quality than the one she demonstrated in previous albums. In some moments, her voice is reminiscent of that of Elizeth Cardoso, still considered by many the best Brazilian singer of all times, and a friend of Lara.[31] For music critic José Ramos Tinhorão, this track is the primary example of Lara's qualities as a singer. According to him, she created in the song a distinctive division of the rhythm, with top-notch vocalizing, but which also positioned her between two very different singers: Clementina de Jesus and Carmen Costa.[32] Lara was "one of the most successful heirs to a Black-Brazilian style of interpretation that has at one end the rough diamond of Clementina de Jesus's voice and in the other the onyx glow of the deep grave vocals of Carmen Costa."[33]

Alguém Me Avisou

Lara's recognition as a singer, however, only came after other famous women lent their voices to her melodies. Above all, it was Maria Bethânia and Gal Costa's rendition of "Sonho Meu," included in Bethânia's album *Álibi* (Alibi) that made Lara known beyond the world of samba. Bethânia then recorded Lara's "Alguém me Avisou" on *Talismã* (Talisman), another hit album which sold more than 800,000 copies. The song, a traditional samba, was composed for Maria Bethânia. The version on *Talismã* is arranged for string instruments and features the voices of two famous *baianos*: Maria Bethânia's brother, Caetano Veloso, and their good friend, Gilberto Gil. The recording, just a year after the *Abertura*—the opening to democracy—gained a symbolic significance since both Gil and Veloso had been exiled to London from 1969 to 1971, and the song talks about a person returning home full of stories to tell. Bethânia included "Sonho Meu," "Alguém me Avisou," and "A Sereia Guiomar" in the lineup of her concerts in the early 1980s. As with "Sonho Meu," which Dona Ivone Lara recorded on her 1979 album *Sorriso de Criança*, Lara included "Alguém me Avisou" on *Sorriso Negro* after the success of Maria Bethânia's rendition.

Lara's is a far more traditional version of the song, with the *cavaquinho* stealing the show, a *cuíca* crying in the background, and female voices singing the chorus. In the last chorus, one can hear hand claps, just as in a *roda de samba*. The song is permeated with Lara's trademark, the beautiful and surprising vocal counterpoints. The melody, however, is not as complex as most of her works. Singer Nilze Carvalho frequently opens her concerts with the tune, which she considers to be the best way of introducing herself. "It is a very simple melody, not one of the usual exquisite melodies that she does. And maybe that is intentional. I also notice that in the last song of the album, *Axé de Ianga.*"

Coincidentally or not, these are the two songs that are most closely related to African heritage, and both were composed by Dona Ivone Lara alone. Pretinho da Serrinha, whose artistic last name is in honor of the neighborhood where he and Lara were raised, jokes that the melody only feels simple because all Brazilians know it by heart "but if you dare trying to write something similar, you will see." For Mart'nália, the song is a call. She claims that, although the lyrics mention Bahia, and the entire piece feels like a homage to the northeastern state, the rhythm is not a *samba de roda*, but a samba with a little bit of Bahia and a lot of Rio de Janeiro, including *samba de terreiro* and *partido-alto*.

Although written for Maria Bethânia, the lyrics seem to be autobiographical. Lara states that "*Alguém me avisou para pisar nesse chão devagarinho*" (Someone told me to step across this floor slowly, which is an expression meaning "watch my step," or "step carefully") when entering the samba world. Juggling the roles expected of a woman in Brazilian society, her full-time job as a social assistant, and the career of songwriter, Lara smoothly navigated these worlds, learning to compartmentalize from a very early age. Pretinho da Serrinha says he made a deal with Lara: to open his concerts with "Alguém me Avisou," for the rest of his life. Because of their similar origin, the lyrics feel autobiographical for him as well.

She sings "*quando eu voltar à Bahia terei muito o que contar*" (when I go back to Bahia I will have a lot to tell) and I sing "*quando eu voltar pra Serrinha*" (when I go back to Serrinha), because I now live in another neighborhood in Rio de Janeiro. But it brings the feeling of your beginnings, a starting point.[34]

The charismatic woman we now know as Dona Ivone Lara was born in Rio de Janeiro on April 13, 1921, and registered as Yvonne da Silva Lara. Her mother, Emerentina Bento da Silva, worked as a seamstress. According to Lara, "she had a very beautiful voice. She was a singer of the rancho Ameno Resedá, but could never fully dedicate herself to music because she needed to make money."[35] Her father, José da Silva Lara, played the seven-string guitar and, during carnival, took part in the parades of Bloco dos Africanos, Ameno Resedá, Flor de Abacate, and other groups that took to the streets of Rio de Janeiro during the festivities. In the early twentieth century, *ranchos* were the main expression of the carnival. They were "groupings of revelers, with string and wind instruments, chanting in unison the *marcha-rancho*, with its music verses alluding to the group."[36] Unlike samba schools, *ranchos* used several wind instruments and formed groups of musicians that resembled small orchestras, including those in which renowned Brazilians such as Pixinguinha and Irineu de Almeida (Irineu Batina) played.[37]

When Lara turned ten years old, she started attending the boarding school Orsina da Fonseca, in the neighborhood of Tijuca. She would only leave the school permanently upon reaching adulthood. Lara spent every week there and left every other weekend to visit her family. Around 300 students attended this all-girl school. The so-called "educational counselors," teachers and principals, monitored the students' routines closely, making sure when classes were over, they had enough activities to keep their minds and bodies busy. The school offered classes in disciplines such as modeling, drawing, painting, engraving, lithography, photography, bookkeeping, typewriting, stenography, typography, brochure making and binding, telegraphy, sewing, and embroidery.[38] Professor Aprígio Gonzaga, who helped craft the curriculum, explained that the institution had to address two types of women: the married women and the single women. To do that, it had to mold students who could be good mothers, wives, and, if necessary, workers, next to their men.[39]

Among the extracurricular activities were physical education and music. Lara's favorites were volleyball and music theory, the latter a prestigious subject. The school had a choir, and the girls selected for it received not only the recognition of the others but also the opportunity to participate in concerts in and outside of the school, at parties, and at events in the city. "At home, we've always heard a lot of radio, and I remember songs by Noel Rosa and other composers of the time. But I think the taste for music, really, started right there in the boarding school," Lara recalls.[40] She had one of the best voices of the choir, and her greatest pride was to be a student of Lucília Villa-Lobos. The *maestra* was married to Heitor Villa-Lobos, considered by many to be Brazil's most celebrated composer of all time. He used to attend the choir presentations to hear classical compositions, including some of his own.

Dona Ivone Lara also found inspiration in another teacher at Orsina da Fonseca, Zaíra de Oliveira. Oliveira was a classically trained soprano who was part of the Coral Brasileiro, which included among its members the legendary Brazilian opera singer Bidú Sayão. She was most active during the 78 rpm era, from 1924 to 1931, when Oliveira recorded a total of twenty-five songs.[41] She is considered one of the greatest singers in the country's history. Her experiences, however, also gave Lara some idea of the challenges she would face as a black woman. In 1921, Oliveira won the competition of the Escola Nacional de Música (National School of Music), the most prestigious music teaching institution in Rio de Janeiro at that time. Nevertheless, being a black woman prevented her from collecting the prize—a trip to Europe.[42] In 1932, Oliveira married Donga, the author of the first recorded samba, "Pelo Telefone."

Lara's songs embody the encounter between samba and classical music. Mart'nália highlights the delicate nature and complexity of her melodies, which have a

> sort of violin all over them as if building a second melody, another music inside the music. Even if it's not there, one can hear a full orchestra of violins, with the main one, a solo. It has an elegance that makes you pay attention to what her intentions are.[43]

Pretinho da Serrinha agrees, adding that it is possible to create another song out of almost all of Lara's pieces, and Leandro Braga says the same about the introductions. "They have such a rich sound material, which can generate other songs, as with 'Sonho Meu.' Even in the introductions, one can already see all the richness of her creativity. In short, all her musical characteristics can be seen easily in the first notes, even without the lyrics."[44] Producer Bertha Nutels remembers that some of Lara's songs did come from parts of others. "Acreditar" (To Believe), for example, one of the most famous works Lara wrote with Delcio Carvalho, came from a vocal counterpoint of another piece of music.[45]

Homemade samba

Gradually, through her dedication to the study of music theory and her attention to the construction of harmony and arrangements of the choir's repertoire, Lara cultivated her love of music. But it was in the biweekly visits to her family that she found her voice. After her mother's death, when Lara was a teenager, she started going to her uncle Dionísio's house in Madureira. The neighborhood is still known as the "cradle of samba" and houses several samba schools and organizations. Dionísio played multiple instruments, and his house was a venue for the best *rodas de choro* of the city. Pixinguinha, Jacob do Bandolim, and Heitor dos Prazeres are some of the biggest names in Brazilian music whom Lara recalls having met in her uncle's backyard. "Samba was very present in my life from an early age," she says, "in the house of my uncles, of my parents, and was not something they perceived as negative; on the contrary—it was appreciated, respected, and even encouraged."

Madureira was a peculiar neighborhood at this time. The so-called rural exodus, when the countryside population began to move to cities, intensified from the 1960s to the 1980s, but in its early stages, some urban areas resisted the change. Madureira was far from Rio de Janeiro's downtown, and its residents worked hard to keep their traditions, including the celebration of carnival in a rural style. In some ways it was as if time had stopped. The region developed slowly, without the underlying processes of gentrification and structural change that the rest of the city faced. There were no movie theaters, opera houses, or big stores. The now-established *Mercadão de Madureira* would only open its doors in 1959. From the 1930s to the 1940s, throughout Lara's childhood and adolescence when she regularly visited her uncle's house, the area offered traditional activities—so traditional that the description Marília Barbosa da Silva writes in her biography of samba composer Silas de Oliveira is hard to translate: "A good *calango* ball, the carnival *blocos* of Seu Zacarias, the *pastorinhas*, the litany of Dona Maria, a *jongo*, a good *pagode*, that is what gathered these people."[46]

However, that was not the reality outside Madureira. During her adolescence, Lara experienced samba's evolution from a cursed rhythm into a national symbol. Hermano Vianna investigates what was behind this turn, which he believes was centered on a quest to forge a national identity. He mentions the commotion that Gilberto Freyre's *The Masters and the Slaves* caused in the early 1930s and the role of the Getúlio Vargas administration. After the Revolution of 1930—which removed from power President Washington Luís, prevented president-elect Júlio Prestes from being inaugurated, and installed Vargas as interim president—the search for unity led the country to a quest for national symbols.[47] Sérgio Cabral, the producer of *Sorriso Negro*, is also a scholar of Brazilian music. He argues that nationalism was part of the political agenda of the 1930s, citing Osvaldo Aranha, former governor of Rio Grande do Sul and minister of Justice and Interior Affairs of the Vargas administration. When attending a concert of the Orquestra Típica Brasileira, conducted by Pixinguinha, Aranha conceded: "I am among those who have always believed in the real national music. I don't believe in foreign influence over our melodies."[48]

When responding to gender and race discrimination, Lara did not seek political confrontation; instead, she prioritized the fulfillment of a broader project in which she maintained a stable job. When *Sorriso Negro* was released, Lara was almost 60 years old. The tardiness of her recognition as a major samba composer was not the result of the market forces alone, but also of the fact that her central objective was to have a formal job and sustain the household without having to rely on her husband or family. She acknowledges loving music above everything, but never refers to it as part of her daily "responsibilities."

When Lara left boarding school, she moved to her aunt Tia Maria's house. The family's meager income, however, was not enough to support all of them and soon her uncle talked her into getting a job. If she didn't find a good one, he would ask for one at the same factory where her cousins worked. That was not what she had envisioned, so she applied to Alfredo Pinto nursing school, which offered her a scholarship. She shared almost all the money with her family. The nursing school presented a real potential for social mobility. The good salaries were attractive, and so was the flexible work schedule. Her uncle Dionísio used to drive ambulances and was a reference for her. He "put food on the table, worked hard, and still made music in his spare time," Lara recalls.[49] It was a path she wanted to follow.

When Lara started studying there, in 1943, the nursing school also offered a certificate of training in psychiatric services. At the time, Rio de Janeiro was still the capital of the country, and courses to train these professionals, called "Assistance to Psychopaths in the Federal District," lasted two years. Among disciplines such as health administration, anatomy, and practical applications of minor surgery, Lara's favorite was medical and social assistance services. For this reason, she decided to attend another course to become a social worker. She was in the first group of students, and the profession was not yet even regulated. After two years, with a diploma in her hands, it was easy to find a job in a hospital of the state health network.

The Institute of Psychiatry of Engenho de Dentro hired Lara as soon as she graduated, in 1947. She remained an employee of the medical facility until she retired in 1977. There, she worked side by side with Dr. Nise da Silveira.[50] It was the early years of what would become a revolution in the treatment of mental diseases. Silveira created a section of occupational therapy and relied on the arts, including music, to understand the psychotic process. Through what she called images of the unconscious, she investigated individual characteristics of patients—or clients, as Silveira preferred to call them—and became a pioneer in the research of the emotional relationship between patients and animals, whom she called co-therapists. Silveira was Lara's supervisor and taught her the importance of dialoguing with families. They worked in a large room and developed several activities, such as dancing, singing, and painting. During this period, her regular meetings with other samba composers became less frequent. Contact with music came mostly from her work at the hospital. Reconciling work with "leisure" had become a difficult task, and one of her strategies was to schedule vacations for February when the carnival parade took place.

During the 1930s and 1940s, the major samba school in the region of Madureira was Prazer da Serrinha. Alfredo Costa, an elegant man with a wispy mustache and sharp eyes, founded it as a powerful family business. He was a great *mestre-sala*, the principal dancer of a samba school, and was also a *pai-de-santo* in the African-Brazilian religion of Candomblé. His wife, Aracy Costa, known as Dona Iaiá, was an influential figure in Candomblé and in the traditional dance of *jongo*. The Costas became a kind of royal family of samba in Rio de Janeiro. Both Alfredo Costa and Iaiá received the award "Samba-Citizen," created by the Union of Samba Schools to honor the most prominent figures of the samba scene. Costa was the president, director, organizer, owner, and *mestre-sala*, occupying pretty much every leadership position in Prazer da Serrinha. It was a well-organized entrepreneurship. Their son, Oscar, was a calm and charming young man. His best friend was Silas de Oliveira, already considered one of the most talented composers of the neighborhood. Oscar's temper was different from the other guys. He would rather talk than party. Lara fell in love. They married in 1947, when she was 26 years old.[51]

Despite her wedding with Oscar—a lower-middle-class man, even if he was part of samba royalty—Lara still didn't feel comfortable relying solely on her career as a samba composer. Those were "the natural limits for a woman," she believed.[52] If her uncle Dionísio served as a model for his ability to combine a formal job with his passion for music, her aunt Maria was a permanent source of discouragement. She did not think the musical universe was the place for Lara. "It was also about going to certain places. She thought the samba environment, always full of alcohol and men, was not for a woman. For her, it would hurt me to be part of it," Lara remembers.[53] Maria's reaction revealed the fears and experiences of the time. Pretinho da Serrinha says that Tia Ira, a contemporary of Lara who also came from one of the founding families of Rio de Janeiro samba schools, used to recall that in her youth she was not even allowed to look out at the street through the window, let alone write songs.[54] Lara never directly challenged these kinds of rules. Her questioning of gender and race inequality was more discreet and gradual.

Meu Fim de Carnaval Não Foi Ruim and Nunca Mais

At the time of the release of *Sorriso Negro*, nonetheless, Brazilian women were at a tipping point. Encouraged by the labor movement, which many of them had joined in the previous years of rapid industrialization, they created community groups with new agendas including progressive goals like universal daycare and higher wages. In the 1970s, associations such as the Movimento do Custo de Vida (Movement of the Cost of Living) demanded a price-freeze for essential goods, wage increases, and agrarian reform, and expanded into the suburbs of São Paulo with the support of both the church and feminists.

Despite her rejection of the label "feminist," Lara's discourses and strategies followed the pace of the movement in Brazil: she proceeded slowly, but surely forward. In *Sorriso Negro*, she distanced herself from partnerships with male composers and wrote lyrics and music for five of the twelve tracks of the album on her own. That, alone, is an imposing narrative of a woman. The wider movement to make samba into a national symbol of Brazil had inflicted even more restrictions on women, who were rarely professional musicians. It gave prominence to "composers, writers, and excellent instrumentalists, making black women's participation and importance in the universe of samba disappear."[55] Women remained limited to the positions of *Tias*, *Baianas*, or muses, "reducing their roles to several stereotypes also reunited around women in general, and black women in particular, because they carry the weight of centuries of slavery, confined to the place of 'ama de leite' (wet nurse), caregiver, cook, and sexual object, among others."[56]

After Lara, Leci Brandão is probably the second name that comes to mind when one thinks about female samba composers. Brandão states that there are so few of them that even for her it is hard to name others. Lara's compositions, in her opinion, have such a strong mark that it is impossible not to notice her unique style. This quality makes her music a statement of female power. "She is an expert when writing a *partido-alto*, but also when writing a romantic, calm song. There is a lyricism which is always present, and it makes her work unique in terms of compositions," Brandão concedes.[57]

The uniqueness and success of Lara as a composer opened an avenue for women in the samba universe. A winding avenue, for sure, but a new path nevertheless. Keeping this in perspective is helpful in recognizing the examples of *resistance by existence* in *Sorriso Negro*. The song "Alguém Me Avisou" references several other women. Rosinha de Valença's presence can be noticed in the arrangements that portray Brazilian folklore through modern lenses. Musician Zé Luis Oliveira observes that the line in the introduction echoes Elis Regina's rendition of João Bosco and Aldir Blanc's "Bala Com Bala."[58] There is also a sorority in the vocal arrangements. Lara sings freely, and it is the female chorus that allows her to do so, sustaining the melody while she does a scat performance, improvising melodic lines in variations of what the mandolin, the soprano saxophone, and the *cuíca* are playing.

"Meu Fim de Carnaval Não Foi Ruim" (The End of My Carnival Was Not Bad) is one of the five songs Lara composed alone for the album. Its lyrics in the first person describe the feelings of someone whose heart had been broken who now sees that loved one regretting having left. The singer is happy at last, the lyrics contend, to be together again with the beloved person who left promising never to come back. "*Mas você não cumpriu e se arrependeu / E voltou exigindo ficar no mesmo lugar*" (But you did not fulfill the promise and felt regret / And came back demanding to be in the same place).[59] The word "demanding" clearly states who is the boss in the relationship: the one who left. However, there is no instance in the lyrics in which it is possible to identify if the narrator is male or female. It is almost like a linguistic trap for the listener, in which, following the general expectations of Brazilian society of the time (and the fact that the singer and composer is a woman), one would almost automatically assume it is a woman telling the story. It is important to remember that this was a time when several Brazilian composers (most prominently, Chico Buarque) were playing with this idea of writing and singing songs from a female perspective. Therefore, it is possible that Lara was singing from a male perspective and that the "alpha" in this relationship was a woman. The decision is on the listener.

"Meu Fim de Carnaval Não Foi Ruim" pairs perfectly with "Nunca Mais" (Never Again), in which the lyrics cause the same effect. There is no way of pointing to the gender of the narrator, another person with a broken heart but, this time, decided not to give in. He/she is denying forgiveness after being cheated and declares: *"Não me convences, para mim não serves mais"* (You can't convince me, you are worthless for me). Another part of the lyrics suggests that that is the voice of a man, since it states that some unidentified person revealed, on the condition of it being kept a secret, *"Que andas de mão em mão"* (That you are promiscuous). However, the expression "andas de mão em mão" presupposes passivity, something close to "you have been in the hands of multiple sexual partners," therefore, for many listeners, it may indicate a reference to a woman. If that is the case, again, the judgment belongs to the listener.

Furthermore, the songs flirt with *pagode*, which Nei Lopes called "the most important musical phenomenon of the 1980s in Brazil."[60] Bira Presidente was at the center of this new trend, a turning point for the samba universe. He was the founder of Fundo de Quintal and of the carnival *bloco* Cacique de Ramos. *Pagode* was a movement of resistance to commercial trends of the time. "People only listened to 'enlatados,' those very commercial songs from the United States and even from Brazil, all of poor quality. It was a tough moment for samba."[61] Then, Beth Carvalho appeared, a young middle-class singer who sang bossa nova. She had been famous since the success of the song "Andança," by Paulinho Tapajós, Danilo Caymmi, and Edmundo Souto, which placed third in the contentious 1968 Festival Internacional da Canção (International Festival of the Song).[62] During the 1970s, she recorded several songs by traditional samba composers, such as Cartola and Nelson Cavaquinho. In the late 1970s, Carvalho started to attend the weekly meetings and *rodas de samba* at Cacique de Ramos, and in 1978, she released the album *De Pé no Chão* (RCA Victor), which opened with "Vou Festejar" (I'll Celebrate), by Edel Ferreira de Lima (Dida), Neoci Dias de Andrade, and Jorge Aragão. The song was one of the most popular at Cacique de Ramos. Jorge Aragão, Almir Guineto, and the Fundo de Quintal group became fixtures in the Brazilian musical scene. Beth Carvalho became known as the "godmother of samba," for having introduced several artists to larger audiences.

It was around that time that Dona Ivone Lara began to attend the events at Cacique de Ramos. It was like being at the backyard of one of the *tias*. "The place was always packed with the greatest sambistas of all times. All that swing, cachaça, beer . . . Suddenly all of the newspapers and tv channels were interested in doing stories about us," remembers Bira Presidente. In 1993, Leci Brandão released the album *Um Ombro Amigo*, for which she recorded "Isso É Fundo de Quintal" (This is Fundo de Quintal), in which she sang "*O que é isso meu amor, venha me dizer / Isso é Fundo de Quintal, é pagode pra valer*" (What is this, my love, tell me / This is Fundo de Quintal, the real *pagode*). Despite the homage, Bira Presidente dislikes the association between the group and *pagode*. For him, the term was nothing but a media creation to explore the trend. "What we sing is traditional samba. Nobody likes to be called *pagodeiro*. We are not that. This term refers to a reunion of people. There are even Japanese connections to this thing. We don't accept this. I will not mistreat someone who says that, but we are not *pagodeiros*." In Rio working-class suburbs, however, many considered the term an honor. It was not only a gathering but a way of resisting the commercialization of the samba schools.[63]

First steps

Long before the 1964 coup d'état, Brazilian women began calling for equality. These gathering energy came to a head when Bertha Lutz created the League for Intellectual Emancipation of Women in 1919 and the Brazilian Federation for Women's Progress, in 1922.[64] Women's suffrage and gender equality in the workplace were at the core of the agenda. In 1932, the Brazilian National Assembly enacted a new constitution, which finally gave women the right to vote and equal labor rights, including a provision to eradicate unequal pay due to sex, age, place of birth, or marital status.[65] However, if this affected Lara as a worker, she continued to be restrained as a samba composer. When showing her first sambas to an audience, she chose to hide her authorship. Her cousin, known as Mestre Fuleiro, sang the songs as if he had composed them. Only many years later did she feel confident enough to state openly that she was the author of the sambas. Fuleiro developed a career of his own and became one of the most acclaimed samba composers of Império Serrano. Lara remembers these episodes with pride, not anger. As someone conscious of her agency, she defended the strategy as a choice, not as an example of her own oppression. "It was a success. He played, and everyone liked, praised, asked where he had gotten the idea. I would stay close, watching that, listening to what they said, and thinking it was all mine. Prejudice never angered me. I was proud to see that the people liked my creations."[66]

She denies any victimization, but the fact that Lara refers to it as prejudice suggests that despite her refusal to feel wronged, she knew such imposed limitations were not right. Her timid demands for space are an example of an individual acting with an enormous degree of what Henri Bergson called *attention a la vie*, a highly conscious emphasis on action in which perception and neural mechanisms work to promote a fast and effective adaptation to reality by combining the surrounding environment with past references.[67] Closely linked to this concept is the assumption that we all participate in several sub-universes which require different attentions, in a continuous but dynamic flow. With Dona Ivone Lara, her strategies of resistance enabled her to reach a position that influenced the following generations. We return to the idea of *resistance by existence*, when there is a conscientious course of action focusing on a future objective, an "in-order-to-motive," in the words of Alfred Schütz; a behavior chosen by the individual, after a proper interpretation of reality, with the intention of reaching a project not yet attained.[68] But even if conceived as an individual project, *resistance by existence* generates an impact in intersubjective understanding, reshaping society's shared knowledge. While navigating the externally imposed limitations to her personal development, Lara not only assumes but also acts according to the comprehension of the other, creating, through her own experience and achievements, a new set of expectations for black women in the musical environment. It is a question not only of adjustment but also of resistance and impact.

Following the publication of Simone de Beauvoir's *The Second Sex*, in 1949, demands for equality grew in Brazil. The accelerated industrialization between the 1960s and 1980s reshaped the organization of the Brazilian family. With an urgent need to increase the labor force, women began their integration into working society.[69] It was also the time of the dictatorship, and the fight for gender equality was relegated to second place as feminists joined the resistance. The groups that emerged in Latin America during the second wave of feminism faced a scenario very different from those in Europe and the United States. They had to compete with other ideologies and find a space inside the Left, which at the time prioritized debates considered to be more urgent, including the fight for democracy and for their lives. However, feminism never disappeared. Feminists who engaged in the armed guerrilla resistance against the regime perceived state terrorism as the most active demonstration of *machismo*.[70]

Mothers were on the frontline. In March 1968, around 300 students went to restaurant Calabouço after a demonstration in downtown Rio de Janeiro. The military police invaded the place and shot two young men, Benedito Frazão Dutra, who died in the hospital, and Edson Luis, whose body was carried throughout the streets of the city to the steps of the city council, at Cinelândia. His death culminated in a series of demonstrations against the military in the entire country. Among the many protest signs, one of the most well-known read: "They killed a student. He could be your son."[71] The words inspired the founding of a women's movement, the União Brasileira de Mães (Brazilian Mothers' Union), with more than 500 affiliated members.[72] On September 12, 1968, in an article titled "The Revolt of the Mothers," the newspaper *Correio da Manhã* described the movement, which intended to gain the support of "all (all with no exception) Brazilian mothers. The objective is one: fight side-by-side with their sons for education reform."[73] Lúcia Rodrigues de Brito, one of the interviewees, stated that the Brazilian political group was stronger than its international counterparts. "Our movement is unprecedented. In France, in the United States, in the entire world, there is a revolt. The mothers are at home. In Brazil, on the contrary, it is instrumental that everyone knows that the mothers are organized. They take to the streets with their children."[74]

The rise of feminism

Months after Edson Luis's death, the dictatorship intensified its oppression with the approval of the Institutional Act Number Five, on December 13, 1968. It suspended all constitutional guarantees, resulting in the institutionalization of torture and censorship.[75] Under these circumstances, the women's movements waned. In an estimate based on data from the

Brazilian Amnesty Committee, founded in 1978, Maria Amélia de Almeida Teles calculates the ratio of women to men in the leftist organizations of resistance to the regime to be roughly 12 percent.[76] Many such groups operated from the same set of perceptions and expectations as did Brazilian society as a whole. The largest Catholic country in the world put family first, and this meant that women were expected to focus on motherhood, marriage, and household duties above all. Outside of these groups, in a political environment in which protests and meetings were prohibited, there was even less space for feminism.

Inside the armed guerrilla groups, women rarely took leadership positions. When it came to military strategy, their primary roles were gathering intelligence and information. Male leaders perceived them as more fragile and less discerning, so their attempts to "masculinize" themselves were frequent. In the Araguaia Guerrilla, for instance, sexual relations were avoided as much as possible.[77] If captured by government agents, they frequently suffered sexual abuse, rape, and torture of the genitals. There were also women working for the dictatorship agencies, but they were similarly deployed. It was common to use couples who pretended to be partners to gather information and to arrest left-wing activists.[78]

If the repression of the government after 1964 and during the 1970s made it impossible for the Brazilian feminist movement to flourish as it had in other countries, the late 1970s and early 1980s emerged as a period of sharp questioning of gender roles in Brazilian society. The United Nations named 1975 the International Women's Year (IWY) and the United Nations Decade for Women was established from

1976 to 1985. The Brazilian women's movements, in general, welcomed the UN initiative as an opportunity to make public the requests that the authoritarian regime prevented from being debated. In January 1979, a women's commission in the Congresso Nacional pela Anistia (National Congress for Amnesty) proposed that the movement to bring political exiles back to Brazil join forces with the feminist movement. It demanded assistance for children and accountability regarding female victims of the regime. In March 1979, around a thousand women united in the Congresso da Mulher (Women's Conference) in São Paulo. In April, the I Conferência Nacional de Mulheres (First National Women's Conference) took place.

After they had engaged in the armed fight against the dictatorship, several of these women created publications and institutions to promote a feminist agenda. Between 1975 and 1980, the feminist newspapers *Nós Mulheres* (We, the Women) and *Brasil Mulher* (Women Brazil) published eight and twenty editions, respectively.[79] Tabloid-sized and printed in black and white, they were financed by the women who edited them and by their sales revenue. There were no ads or sponsors. The angle and topics of the stories were defined in meetings that resembled those of guerrilla groups where some of the editors were militants: heated debates that could last for days.[80] Labor rights were still a central part of the coverage, but abortion, sex, orgasm, and the division of domestic labor were also included.

The creation of several new political parties added feminism to the debate. Opposition parties such as Partido Trabalhista Brasileiro (PTB), Partido do Movimento Democrático Brasileiro (PMDB), Partido Democrático Trabalhista (PDT), and Partido dos Trabalhadores (PT), incorporated women's rights into the agenda. In 1986 the so-called Bancada do Batom (Lipstick Bench) comprised twenty-six congresswomen and was fundamental for the approval of the 1988 national constitution of Brazil.[81] Domestic violence and the legalization of abortion entered the debate, although this did not result in any change in legislation.

Also in 1979, the Amnesty Law was approved, pardoning civilians and military personnel for all the crimes committed during the dictatorship. Several Brazilian intellectuals, teachers, artists, workers, and people who the regime considered to be menacing were finally able to return to the country. In 1980, the publication of *Memórias das Mulheres do Exílio* was an attempt at narrating women's collective memories of the exile. On the book's cover, the words *das mulheres* (of women) appear forcefully in the title, a way of demonstrating that they were not included even among the already peripheral group of exiles. Whenever discussions of race or gender were brought to the table, they were set aside by the more significant and urgent preoccupation with the end of the dictatorship. Such debates only gained strength when a democratic voting system became a reality.

Angela Neves-Xavier de Brito investigates the importance of feminist organizations in the context of the exile community and of the different countries to which they fled.[82] She separates two "waves" of exiles: the 1964 group, who moved right after the coup d'état, mainly to other Latin American countries, and the 1968 group, who looked for destinations in Europe and Africa. The first group of women faced a return to the previous status they held before they had engaged in political activism. According to the author, this was due to the structure of Latin American leftist civic organizations, which kept women in an inferior position with no possibility of incorporating a new identity. With the second group, on the other hand, it was a different story. In Europe, the process of building a new consciousness on the part of Brazilian women began to emerge. Brito claims that "reflection on the conditions of oppression of women could only be done in exile and especially in societies whose social conditions favored its appearance. It could never have been done in societies such as Brazil or Chile, imbued with patriarchal values."[83]

In societies with a vast Catholic majority such as Brazil, the development of the feminist movement encountered several challenges. Dona Ivone Lara, however, was a unique case. On the one hand, she believes that her blackness was partly responsible for the lateness of her recognition as an artist. On the other hand, her racial background provided her family with a legacy of African matriarchal societies. The image of African women as strong and combative matriarchs, able to overcome obstacles in the struggle for their lives and those of their children, is connected to black female identity not only in Africa but also in the countries of the diaspora.[84] The matriarchal African structure took hold at various points of Lara's life. In Candomblé, it is the *mãe-de-santo* that holds the position of higher prestige and power, being the spiritual head of the religion.[85]

It would not be an exaggeration to say that the traditional African matriarchal structure transposed itself onto Lara's relations with relatives, neighbors, and friends. Being a black woman undoubtedly carried a heavy burden of oppression, but in some of the sub-universes that Lara navigated, it could otherwise confer some authority. Singer Mart'nália is the daughter of samba composer Martinho da Vila, a good friend of Lara all her life. She frequented her house often, and Lara called her *netinha* (granddaughter) so that for a long time Mart'nália believed they were related. This relationship inspired her with the idea that there were no natural boundaries for women or blacks. "It has never been a question for me. I thought we were all naturally capable of anything."[86]

When talking about the time when Fuleiro was presenting Lara's songs while she was studying social assistance, composer Leci Brandão frames these actions as the forging of historical shifts, such as Lara being the first woman to compose a *samba-enredo*. Brandão asserts that what Mart'nália experienced will echo through several generations because Lara's music is timeless. "When Dona Ivone Lara is on a stage, there is a light, a force that, for black girls, can be an example. It is a history of female protagonism which can serve as inspiration and as an example of a black woman who succeeds. An example of strength and creativity."[87]

Part 2

Faces

For Elifas Andreato, the process of creating the cover design has been the same for the more than 300 albums he has illustrated. He listens to the songs, talks to the artist, and drafts a series of ideas. His primary objective is to reflect what the music aspires to express, while at the same time inviting the listener to take a step further, imagining the social and political implications of the work, even if they are not explicitly there. It is almost as if he were thinking a little bit like a composer, making suggestions and additions to what the album entails. Andreato started applying his artistic talent to works of music during the military regime, in the zenith of the repression, right after the Institutional Act Number Five. He designed covers for artists such as Paulinho da Viola, Martinho da Vila, Clementina de Jesus, Zeca Pagodinho, Elis Regina, Gonzaguinha, Chico Buarque, and Clara Nunes. His colorful drawings protested the dictatorship in subtle ways that did not directly confront agents of censorship; the perspicacity allowed his artworks to make their way to the stores.[1]

In the cover art for Paulinho da Viola's *Nervos de Aço* (1973), the singer appears with his face covered in tears, holding dying flowers in his hands.[2] The album is full of emotional lyrics, most of them about lost loves.[3] The second track, "Comprimido," describes the daily challenges of preserving love in a time of silence and violence. It narrates the suicide of a man who suddenly started pushing his wife away. She thinks he is having an affair; they fight, he beats her. They end up at a police station, where the detective explains that he cannot do much, since "nobody can judge the matters of the heart." The man seems to keep a secret that turns him into another person, a dark version of himself, unknown to his wife. The woman tells the story to a police investigator and finally states that it all seemed to be related to the fact that he spent a lot of time listening to a samba by Chico Buarque about daily life.

It is a reference to the song "Cotidiano," which narrates the life of a housewife who, according to her husband, does the same things, the same way, every day.[4] The day starts when she wakes him up punctually at 6 a.m. and ends with her by the door at 6 p.m., waiting for him to return. The song was released in 1971 and called attention to a feminist complaint: the confinement of women to the domestic realm. In the context of this track and the other song it references, seeing Paulinho da Viola's crying, fragile face on the cover of the album gives "Comprimido" and the album's other love songs another layer of interpretation, one that questions gender expectations.

For context, it is worth noting that not all of Andreato's work was so subtle or his activism so subdued. His poster for the theater play *Mortos Sem Sepultura* (Death Without Burial), by Jean-Paul Sartre, showed a man in a *pau-de-arara*, an instrument of torture frequently used during the Brazilian dictatorship, in which a pole is placed behind the victim's knees while the ankles and wrists are tied together. It causes acute muscle pain, headaches, and psychological trauma. In the background of the illustration stands an officer with a swastika band on his arm. He wears sunglasses, and his entire figure is in black and white, completing the dark scene.

At the time of *Sorriso Negro*, in the early 1980s, Adreato had over a decade of experience with album covers. Born in the state of Paraná in 1946, the artist and graphic designer was then living in Rio de Janeiro and was friends with many musicians. He recalls that, for him, creating and supervising the artwork for the cover of *Sorriso Negro* was an extraordinary opportunity to reflect the aims of the feminist movement, since Lara was at a particularly powerful moment in her career. More than 15 years after her debut, in an official carnival parade in 1965, she was finally recognized as a pioneering figure outside the samba world as well as inside it. "Everyone was talking about the fact that she was a woman in such a masculine world," Adreato explains.[5]

> Dona Ivone Lara has this incredible capacity to seduce. As a composer, she is exceptional, especially as a melodist. What I wanted was to see if I could graphically portray the content of the album, which, for me, had her trademarks: beautiful melodies and elaborated verses. I thought the cover was great in revealing the content of the LP while, at the same time, showing her powerful figure.[6]

Iolanda Huzak photographed Lara for the cover and back of the album. Ruth Freihof supervised the work, and Alexandre Huzak signed the final art. It brings more than just a picture: Lara's face, name, and chest are in different tones of brown, beige, white, and black. Her smile, simultaneously contained and open, is bright red. "The mouth. It was all about the mouth. I did it because of her sweet voice, but also because the title of the album and the song are so strong and evident that this needed to be present in the cover."[7]

Producer Sérgio Cabral and Andreato knew each other from the music business but also from political activism. Andreato contends that the early 1980s were a time when they could finally move away from fighting the regime to address other seminal questions of Brazilian society:

> Sorriso Negro was a choice, a progression of what I had been doing with other artists, such as Martinho da Vila, and Paulinho da Viola. So, yes, there was a political statement in the mouth, in that scream. The fight against the regime demanded a lot from everyone. At that point we were starting to look at other questions, such as gender; it was a moment full of challenges. There was a feeling that everyone should give her what she was worth, being a pioneer and a very talented composer.[8]

He recalls that around the time of the production of *Sorriso Negro*, he worked with journalist Fernando Faro at TV Globo, the biggest Brazilian television network. Faro recorded a show with composer Bucy Moreira, following his style of close-ups and long shots. According to Andreato, the show did not air because TV Globo's general director of programming, José Bonifácio de Oliveira Sobrinho, known as Boni, decided that Moreira's teeth looked too bad for television. Outraged by what they considered to be censorship, Andreato and Faro quit. Moreira was the grandson of Tia Ciata, the host of the reunions in which the first sambas were created. "I think this incident was crucial in my process of creating this cover for Dona Ivone Lara."[9]

Names

On the cover of *Sorriso Negro*, the name of the artist appears as Dona Yvonne Lara. On the record sleeve, there are places where it is written the same way and others where one reads Yvonne Lara or Dona Ivone Lara. Warner Music Brazil's full report states that the artist's legal name and her display name are both D. Yvonne Lara. On all other albums except for *Sorriso Negro,* it was spelled Dona Ivone Lara. The removal of the "Y," present in her certificate of baptism but not in the Portuguese alphabet, was a suggestion of producer Adelzon Alves, who had worked with her on the previous albums and to whom she dedicates *Sorriso Negro.* The choice turned her into an even more "authentic" representation of Brazilianess. This dispute between Y and I is a symbol of a tension that had started decades earlier: should Brazil embrace the "Americanization" of its culture or repel it to save its traditions and roots?

In the late 1950s, while international tourists packed nightclubs in Rio de Janeiro, a group of wealthy young musicians started meeting at singer Nara Leão's house to do "as amateurs what nightclub musicians had been doing professionally for a while, mimicking the Americans: the samba sessions that allowed them to play samba in a jazz style, with freedom to improvise and with no preoccupation with time."[10] Music critic José Ramos Tinhorão, who would later write the critique of *Sorriso Negro* for the newspaper *Jornal do Brasil*, became the most famous detractor of this genre invented by João Gilberto and Tom Jobim, stating it was nothing more than a slight modification of samba. "The traditional samba was very straight, set, marked in that two-four meter. João Gilberto's great invention was to slow down the time. It is like a drip that does not fall all the time precisely. Bossa nova is the rhythm of the water drip," he argued in a debate with Hermínio Bello de Carvalho, Lara's partner in "Unhas."[11] Carvalho responded to Tinhorão that

> the invention of bossa nova has nothing to do with another type of samba. It is samba, yes. It is Brazilian, yes. Tom [Jobim] is a great composer. I am not saying that just because I think so. He was revered by a partner of mine: Alfredo da Rocha Vianna, Pixinguinha. I follow Pixinguinha's lead. We have to recognize this. I listen to Tom with immense pleasure.[12]

In the late 1960s and 1970s, resistance to what many perceived as US penetration into the Brazilian market gained the support of both right-wing groups who defined the nationalist policies of the military regime and leftists who claimed it was necessary to fight Uncle Sam's influence. The demonstration against the electric guitar—which had become a symbol of Yankee imperialism—is one example. In July 1967, Gilberto Gil, Geraldo Vandré, Elis Regina, Jair Rodrigues, and other stars of Brazilian music joined more than 300 demonstrators in the streets of São Paulo.[13] Nara Leão and Caetano Veloso saw the protest as fascist, similar to how Víctor Jara felt when antagonizing his peers and embracing rock and roll in Chile.[14] The producer of *Sorriso Negro*, Sérgio Cabral, was a juror for many of the music festivals of TV Record and was among the ones who supported the protest:

> You see, today I can make a self-criticism. I sided with the demonstration, which I now see as a ridiculous thing. Of course, shortly after I realized it, I became a record producer, and I finally found it silly to be against the electric guitar. It is a stupid thing, right? It is silly. But, folks, for us nationalists, leftists, music could not be invaded by what came from outside, and the electric guitar was a symbol of this invasion.[15]

The "silly" fight, however, did not prevent Cabral from defending an amalgamation of samba and bossa nova.

In 1928, Mário de Andrade suggested that music was the most robust creation of the Brazilian race.[16] It was natural, then, that this claim to national identity became a point of contention during the dictatorship.[17] In 1965, the Nelson Oliveira Pesquisas de Mercado (Nopem), started keeping track of record sales in Brazil. The Nopem produced annual reports on sales; although they offer data on too narrow a section of the complex music market of Brazil at the time, these numbers can help to illustrate the fluctuations of samba sales. In a study published in 2008, scholar Eduardo Vicente investigated the segmentation of this sector from 1965 to 1999. Using the Nopem numbers, he argues that there was an "emergence and consolidation of the generation of composers and interpreters of the 1960s that until now works as the most important reference of the decade."[18] Vicente referred to figures such as Chico Buarque, Gilberto Gil, and Caetano Veloso, which he classified as Música Popular Brasileira (MPB).

According to Vicente's interpretation of the Nopem numbers, bossa nova was present in eight out of the fifty top sellers of 1965: *A bossa é nossa* by Miltinho; *Dois na bossa* by Elis & Jair Rodrigues; *Quem te viu, quem te vê* by Chico Buarque; *Minha namorada* by Os Cariocas; *Carcará* by Nara Leão; *Arrastão* by Edu Lobo; *Inútil paisagem* by Nana Caymmi; and *Reza* by Tamba Trio.[19] From the fifty top-selling albums in that same year, fifteen were foreign, seventeen romantic, eight MPB, and six samba. In 1981, when *Sorriso Negro* was released, eleven were international, sixteen romantic, fifteen MPB, and four samba. The zenith of international music was in the 1970s and its decline in the 1980s and 1990s. Samba, on the other hand, was growing slowly in the 1960s.[20] Elza Soares's album *A bossa negra* (The black bossa), released in 1961, is an example of the discontent of *sambistas* with this new reality, in which "traditional" Brazilian music was replaced by other rhythms.[21]

The expansion of bossa nova and *jovem guarda* made the 1960s rough for traditional samba composers. The new generation of music stars, including Nara Leão, Elis Regina, Gilberto Gil, Caetano Veloso, and Maria Bethânia, continued to record sambas. However, albums of sambistas like Dona Ivone Lara, Nelson Cavaquinho, and Cartola never made it to the best-sellers list. In 1972, Amaury Monteiro lamented at *O Globo* the end of traditional samba, stating that for a good *sambista*, "Rio's night is the shortest path" to survival.[22] Indeed, many artists were able to secure some of the few available opportunities from nightclubs in Rio. Lara did some memorable concerts in these venues, to audiences packed with samba lovers, including influential musicians, artists, and journalists. In short, it was there that she found many of the opinion makers who helped her become a known figure outside the samba community in Rio's "north zone" (*Zona Norte*). "When I did my first concert at the nightclub Monsieur Pujol, in Ipanema," she says, "people started to know me there even more than in Madureira."[23]

She became a fixture at Osvaldo Sargentelli's nightclubs, including *Sambão*, one of the most popular clubs in Rio de Janeiro at the time. In 1970, with producer Adelzon Alves, Sargentelli decided to unite on one album, titled *Sargentelli e o Sambão*, the most celebrated names of samba who frequently played at the bar. It was the first time Lara recorded her voice on an album. With the track "Sem cavaco não" (Not without a *cavaco*), written together with Mano Décio da Viola, Lara set her foot in the history of samba. In "Agradeço a Deus" (I Thank God), Sargentelli gave her the title "Dona," although she tried to refuse it. Before the song starts, he asks Roberto Carlos, Wilson Simonal, Elis Regina, and several other major names of Brazilian music to pay attention to "Dona" Ivone. Lara recalls

> the album was excellent, but when we heard it together, Sargentelli and Adelzon called me and said, "Dona Ivone. From now on your stage name is Dona Ivone Lara." I think out of respect because they liked my work, but I said: "Dona? I am too young for that." But they insisted and also decided to change the spelling of Yvonne, which became Ivone, to make it easier for the audience. Well, it worked.[24]

Adelzon Alves remembers that when he sent her first album, *Samba minha verdade, samba minha raiz*, from 1978, to the label—he did it without her knowledge. "It went as 'Dona,' which she did not want," he recalls. "And the first thing we saw in the news was an article by Sérgio Cabral talking about exactly that, weaving a thousand compliments to her and mentioning that the detail [calling her Dona] had really been necessary, attracted attention."[25]

In 1974 Adelzon Alves produced another collective album, *Quem Samba Fica? Fica* (The ones who dance the samba stay? They do). It featured "Agradeço a Deus" again, closing the album, and "Tiê," Lara's first song, composed with her cousin Mestre Fuleiro when she was 12 years old. Alves went on to produce Lara's first two albums, *Samba, minha verdade, samba, minha raiz* and *Sorriso de Criança* (1979). Lara also became a regular at the concert *Noitada de Samba* (Samba Night), which took place weekly in the late 1970s at the Teatro Opinião, in Copacabana. The theater was known for being a place of resistance to the dictatorship. It welcomed the greatest names of Brazilian music at the time, and every Monday night was reserved for samba. It was a time of transition, in which the "national rhythm" was gradually losing out to bossa nova and Tropicália, genres that borrowed from jazz and rock and roll.[26]

The return to writing her name with a Y is the initial sign of the shift in *Sorriso Negro*, Lara's first album without Alves's signature. Sérgio Cabral, her new producer, was an experienced journalist, writer, and musical producer, having curated albums by Baden Powell and Cartola. Cabral met Lara when she performed in the concert Unidos do Pujol, in 1974, which he codirected with Albino Pinheiro. At first listen, it appears that Cabral had kept close to what Alves had done, with sambas and partnerships with Delcio Carvalho, Hermínio Bello de Carvalho, Silas de Oliveira, Bacalhau, and Jorge Aragão. That was not at all the case, though. The repertoire, as well as the two special guests, Maria Bethânia and Jorge Ben, marked a clear departure from Lara's earlier albums. Bethânia and Ben were celebrities and two of the most influential representations of MPB (Brazilian Popular Music). Cabral's idea was to broaden Lara's audience beyond a samba-oriented market.

Os Cinco Bailes da História do Rio

Partners have always been a critical part of Dona Ivone Lara's musical endeavors. She never liked to write the lyrics and found in melodies her greatest strength. The world of samba also invites such connections. It is in meetings and *rodas* full of people from various communities that many songs are born. Whether they originate in improvisations or in rigorous processes of composition, most of the *sambas-enredo* are the result of the work of two or more composers. This was the case for "Conferência de São Francisco" (São Francisco's Conference), also known as "A Paz Universal" (Universal Peace), which Silas de Oliveira wrote with Mano Décio da Viola for the samba school Prazer da Serrinha in 1946. The community was ready, knew the lyrics, and was enthusiastic about the finale of the carnival parade. However, the president of the samba school, Alfredo Costa, Lara's controversial father-in-law, decided at the last minute that they would instead present "Alto da Colina" (Top of the Hill). For Costa, it was a way of challenging the imposition that all samba schools embrace nationalistic topics, inherited from the Estado Novo dictatorial regime. For Oliveira, nevertheless, it was an insult. After the episode, he and other members of Prazer da Serrinha decided to found the Grêmio Recreativo Império Serrano.

A former Portuguese teacher, Oliveira is still considered one of the greatest composers Brazil has ever had. In 2003, the newspaper *O Globo* asked seventy personalities of the samba world to name the best *samba-enredo* of all time. Oliveira's "Heróis da Liberdade" (Heroes of Freedom) got the first place. His "Aquarela Brasileira" (Brazilian Watercolor) placed third, and his partnership with Dona Ivone Lara and Bacalhau, "Os Cinco Bailes da História do Rio," fourth.[27]

Oliveira used to sit at home and read history books, alone, researching to write the *sambas-enredo*. Later, his friends would arrive for some drinks and to collaborate. Rumor has it that Oliveira gave partnerships away, adding the name of his companions to his songs as thank-you gifts for drinks.[28] For the 1965 carnival competition, Oliveira decided to work with his close friend, Bacalhau. For the first time, all samba schools were required to focus on the same topic: the 400th anniversary of Rio de Janeiro. One day, at home, relaxed, and having drunk a little too much, Oliveira and Bacalhau got stuck in the lyrics and the melody. Lara arrived, saluted the two men, and started humming over what they had. She hated the idea of writing lyrics about a previously determined topic or following a synopsis. It felt like a straightjacket. "I always preferred the melodies," she declared, "and it was no different this time. For me, music is where the real challenge is. To make a beautiful melody, that everybody likes and makes them feel things. To be inspired by it, that is the root of the song."[29] The result of her partnership with the two men was "Os Cinco Bailes da História do Rio."

The lyrics describe the five major balls of the city's history. It starts in 1585 when Rio celebrated its twentieth anniversary. Then, it travels to the moving of the Brazilian capital from Salvador to Rio, in 1763; the acclamation of Dom João VI as king of Portugal, Brazil, and Algarves, in 1818; the ball of Brazil's independence, in 1822; and the last ball of the empire, in 1889. But symbolically, this samba will never be remembered as a narrative of Brazilian monarchs' tendency to party. Instead, it will always be a feminist anthem. It was the first time a woman composed a *samba-enredo* for a major school. Império Serrano and its group marched along Avenue Presidente Vargas, close to Candelária Church, in heavy, expensive, beautifully crafted costumes. It was clear that the school had come to win. Lara recalls that one of the directors of the branch of composers of the school stated Império had been born launching novelties, and that it was very fond of continuing to bring new things to each carnival.[30] That year, Lara was the new thing.

Nevertheless, the samba school Salgueiro also had its innovations, including the use of new materials in its costumes. It challenged the pattern of telling a chapter of Rio de Janeiro's history by doing it through *The Aeneid*. The work of Fernando Pamplona and Joãosinho Trinta, then an unknown designer, was so groundbreaking that many traditionalists demanded that the audience boo it.[31] Nobody did. Salgueiro won with ten points more than Império Serrano, the vice-champion of the 1965 carnival. Musically, however, Império Serrano prevailed. It is "Os Cinco Bailes da História do Rio," not "História do Carnaval Carioca—Eneida" that is still remembered and sung in *rodas de samba* today. Dona Ivone Lara's pioneering role on the song put her in a different position in the samba universe. From that moment on, she became officially recognized as a top-notch songwriter, an artist who was part of the community and of the history of the association. She was also a source of inspiration for black women who were frequently told that certain roles were unattainable for them.

Zé Luiz do Império Serrano, a composer of the samba school, states that during the early part of Lara's career, it was unthinkable for a woman to write music. The environment was very misogynistic, and he doubts that she would have reached the same prominence without her cousin Fuleiro, who was much respected in samba. He told me in an interview that Lara "started off writing 'Os Cinco Bailes da História do Rio,' an instant classic, the big champion."[32] I reminded him that Salgueiro had won that year and he laughed at the mistake, saying that, for him, "Os Cinco Bailes" would always be the great winner. Pretinho da Serrinha explains that just from the introduction one can already tell that it is a different kind of samba. "It is absurd, impressive. It moves from major to minor unexpectedly; it is just amazing. Honestly, I would say that 70% of the richness of this song is in the melody. The lyrics are ok, nothing special. But the melody follows a surprising line," as unpredictable as its author.[33]

In *Sorriso Negro*, the song is very different from the one Império Serrano performed. The female choir resembles a samba school parade when the audience sings along. On the album, Lara offers a much more intimate form. The *surdo* invites the tambourines and, together, they start a rich samba pattern which dialogues with Lara's "la la ia." Again, the woodblock replaces the agogo bell. There is a sad feeling in the first part, with a minor key structure counterpointed by the seven-string guitar. The lyrics accompany the downhearted sentiment, and the singer asks that the popular celebration bring joy: "*Carnaval, doce ilusão / Dê-me um pouco de magia*" (Carnival, sweet illusion / Give me some magic). The major keys dominate the second part when the lyrics narrate the five balls. In the third part, the seven-string guitar does "baixarias," a counterpoint and accompaniment technique typical of the *choro* rhythm. At the end of the song, the same patterns of the introduction are back, in an outro that recalls the cyclical history of Brazil.

Adeus de um Poeta

Silas de Oliveira was born in 1916 and lived his entire life in the neighborhood of Serrinha, in Madureira, "the cradle of samba." The street where he lived most of his childhood, Rua Maroim, is now called Rua Compositor Silas de Oliveira. Born into a conservative family—his father was a teacher and a Protestant pastor—he only discovered samba because of his friendship with Oscar Costa, Lara's future husband and the son of Alfredo Costa, president of samba school Prazer da Serrinha. Alfredo was also a *pai-de-santo*, and the rehearsals of the samba school took place in his *terreiro*. Mãe Tereza, mother of Mestre Fuleiro and Lara's aunt, was one of the most respected women in the *jongo* presentations.[34]

The word *jongo* comes from *dongo* or *kimbundu*, one of the Bantu languages. It borrows a great deal from the African language, including the names of different kinds of drums and words such as *candongueiro*, *cuíca*, *gungunar*, and *zambi*, which derive from the idioms of Congo and Angola and are frequently used in *jongo* ceremonies.[35] In an interview about Lara's career, percussionist and samba composer Wilson das Neves paid tribute to the fact that she was also a great instrumentalist, playing the *cavaquinho* tuned as a mandolin, something very unusual for a woman in the samba environment.[36] Samba also embraces African-Brazilian religions, and in Candomblé, for instance, one does not see women playing or singing. These are men's roles. Therefore, it is yet one more territory in which she became a pioneer.[37]

During 27 years dedicated to the genre of *samba-enredo*, Silas de Oliveira wrote at least nineteen songs for three different samba schools: Prazer da Serrinha, Império Serrano, and Império do Samba, a school based in Santos, São Paulo. He wrote four of them alone, ten with Mano Décio, and the others with different partners. The only one with Dona Ivone Lara was "Os Cinco Bailes da História do Rio." For Lara, it was also the symbol of her friendship with Oliveira.

In *Sorriso Negro*, "Adeus de Um Poeta" received the kind of attention to detail that Silas typically applied to his songs. The *cavaquinho* embellishes the background; the seven-string guitar does rich counterpoints, while tambourines keep the background patterns that support the vocals. Lara states, at the end of the song, that "*Este samba é uma homenagem ao compositor Silas de Oliveira, poeta maior do Império Serrano*" (This samba is a homage to composer Silas de Oliveira, the greatest poet of Império Serrano). Then, heightening the tension of the musical patterns, she exchanges places with the female choir and finally joins it. It feels like a chant of compassion, in which her peers embrace her in this difficult moment, recalling what had happened almost a decade before, when she lost her friend and partner.

The year of 1972 was a tough one for Silas de Oliveira. His samba for that carnival received a grade zero from the jury and was not selected to represent the school in the parade. One of his friends, Mirinho, reveals that he never again talked to the board of the school or the jurors who, according to him, had "destroyed Silas."[38] Oliveira refused to go to the parade and reacted to daily life bitterly, something very unlike him. On May 20th of that same year, he went to a *roda de samba* thinking of getting some extra money to be able to buy some books for one of his daughters.[39] He sang "Meu Drama" (My Drama), "Heróis da Liberdade," and "Os Cinco Bailes da História do Rio," which was to close the presentation. That night, he reached even the highest notes, which he normally avoided. Delcio Carvalho supposedly said the last words Oliveira heard: "Wow, Silas, you are singing like a bird."[40] After singing the last song, Oliveira sat down, and his friends were still talking to him when his body suddenly lurched forward. He had suffered a fatal heart attack.[41]

Besides "Sorriso Negro," "Adeus de um Poeta" is the only song included in *Sorriso Negro* which Dona Ivone Lara did not write. The author, Tião Pelado, describes the respect and pride the entire samba community felt for Oliveira and the suffering caused by his death. In the song, he addresses the musician directly, "*Tu foste em passo firme em linha reta / Um dos mais perfeitos poetas*" (You were at a steady pace in a straight path / One of the most perfect poets). Silas de Oliveira's death, at the age of 55, was devastating for the samba community. Although he was shy and humble, Oliveira had many followers and friends, who revered his talent and admired his honesty. The May 22, 1972, edition of newspaper *O Globo* described his funeral at Irajá's Cemetery, attended by more than 2,000 people, as a demonstration of his importance to the community.

> Natal's hoarse voice sang the first verses of "Heróis da Liberdade," "*Passava a noite, vinha o dia / o sangue do negro corria . . .*" (The night passed, the day came / the blood of the black man ran) starting the most dramatic moment of the funeral. . . . Soon, the heavy silence that followed the prayer was replaced by the singing of all the samba musicians, at a slower pace than the one which is usually heard on the avenue, but of equal strength; "he died in a *roda de partido-alto*, just like he wished," were the words Cartola, from Mangueira, used in trying to comfort the widow.[42]

Some of the musicians who attended the ceremony said that it rained, and the storm expressed the sadness and tears of the people of the northern zone of Rio de Janeiro, who faced insurmountable loss.

Delcio Carvalho remembers Silas de Oliveira's funeral quite well. He recalled that Lara was one of those most shocked by the loss. "She was sad, crying a lot. As if she could not believe what was happening."[43] Carvalho was young but already respected in the samba community. Lara's husband, Oscar, approached him and asked for help. He said he loved Lara very much and could not bear to see her as devastated. "Oh, Delcio, I do not know what will happen to her, full of melodies with no one to write the lyrics. Now, without Silas, her world will be just sadness. You might as well come by and talk to her a little, right? I hear you've been writing some beautiful sambas. What do you think?"[44] It was an invitation he could not refuse. They started meeting every Saturday when Lara was not working. Carvalho was delighted with the melodies she showed him. Together they played, sang, and, gradually, formalized what would be the main partnership of their careers. Bertha Nutels recalls that Delcio Carvalho was attracted to Império Serrano because of Oliveira, whom he considered an awe-inspiring genius, but he developed his talent most fully with his "mystical" partnership with Lara.

Me Deixa Ficar

Like Lara, Delcio Carvalho also came from a musical environment. Born in Campos dos Goytacazes, in the northern area of the state of Rio de Janeiro, he was the son of a saxophonist at the Sociedade Musical Lira de Apolo.[45] The group was founded in 1870 and is still active, performing at public events around the country. However, this did not translate into glamour or money for the family. As a boy, Carvalho came to work as a sugarcane cutter. He began his career singing in small dance clubs in Campos and moved to the capital soon after finishing his military service. He liked music and decided to try living as a singer and composer. At first, he performed at concerts and bars in Duque de Caxias, and, in 1970, at the age of 31, joined the branch of composers of samba school Império Serrano. There, he became closer to his idol, Silas de Oliveira. "He was simply crazy about Silas. Delcio thought of him as a supreme genius. He also liked Mestre Fuleiro very much, and they used to go to bars in the area all the time. He was a people person, and his greatest pleasure was to listen to stories," recalls Bertha Nutels, his producer from 1976 until Carvalho's death, in 2013.[46]

Carvalho was Lara's major musical partner. For those who have listened to some of their songs together, it is hard to explain the connection. The lyricism present in Lara's melodies finds perfect resonance in Carvalho's words. Together, they composed their greatest hits. Lara used to joke that she had stopped counting their collaborations. "Sonho Meu" (My Dream) is the most famous one, but there were many others, including "Acreditar" (To Believe), "Minha verdade" (My Truth), "Alvorecer" (Dawn), and "Nasci para sonhar e cantar" (I Was Born to Dream and to Sing). Their writing process varied, but usually, Lara would show him the music, and he would add the lyrics.

In the early 2000s, when working on my first book about Lara's role as a pioneer of samba, I interviewed Carvalho several times. He told me about this process and how mesmerizing it was, even for them. "She normally writes the melody first and then shows me. I am always amazed at how clear her music is for me. It tells me exactly what she wanted to say with each note. With that in mind, I write the lyrics. When I show her, she always says that I find out precisely what she had envisioned."[47] Lara confirms:

> With Delcio a funny thing happens. He listens to the melody, and it seems as if he gets inspired to write the lyrics immediately. It is an extraordinary thing. We were always looking at each other as if appreciating each other's existence. It never happened that I would listen to one of his lyrics and be unsure, thinking it was bad or not exactly what I had expected. I loved all of them.[48]

Pretinho da Serrinha recalls Carvalho telling him that he did not go to Lara's house religiously every Saturday for no reason. It was work. Bertha Nutels jokes that Lara was a great cook and, for this reason, many people would go to her house, including Delcio. But it was far from his primary interest. She summarizes: "it was a mystical connection, unexplainable."[49] Musician Leandro Braga contends that there is no way of separating Lara from Delcio Carvalho, as their music has a very powerful identity. However, the union was not a balanced one. "In any partnership, music imposes itself on the lyrics: one can notice a bad song quickly, while one can hide mediocre lyrics for a while. Besides that, she is very solid as an interpreter. A beautiful black woman, big, smiling, with a very particular timbre. It is troublesome to sing her songs after she does."[50]

Carvalho was undoubtedly the most frequent of Lara's musical partners. However, on *Sorriso Negro*, only two of their songs are present: "A Sereia Guiomar" and "Me Deixa Ficar" (Let Me Stay). Both are very melodic sambas, but "Me Deixa Ficar" feels way closer to a *pagode*. A trombone does several counterpoints to the vocal melodies, while percussion and strings dominate the first part of the tune. The female choir almost whispers the lyrics, in a very soft dynamic. They seem to be singing very close to the microphone and Lara's voice prevails sometimes singing before the bar line.

In comparison to Lara's previous albums, the two partnerships with Carvalho felt short. On *Samba, minha verdade, samba minha raiz*, there were six, and on *Sorriso de Criança*, seven of them. One of Lara's biographers attributes the lack of their collaborative songs on *Sorriso Negro* to the fact that Carvalho had recently released his solo album *Canto de um Povo*, which included "Sonho Meu," "Acreditar," "Alvorecer," and "Vai na Paz." Besides that, his solo record included songs with other partners, such as Noca da Portela, Barbosa da Silva, and Flávio Moreira.[51] Lara was not pleased. If Carvalho, who was "extremely jealous of his partner could commit these little (and healthy) musical treasons, Ivone also found she had the right to 'fool around.'"[52] Ultimately, however, she ended up not fooling around too much. Besides "Os Cinco Bailes da História do Rio," an almost two-decade-old collaboration with Silas de Oliveira and Bacalhau, the album only included two other collaborations: "Tendência," cowritten with Jorge Aragão, and "Unhas," cowritten with Hermínio Bello de Carvalho.

Unhas

In 1965, while Dona Ivone Lara made history as the first woman to author an official *samba-enredo*, Bello de Carvalho helped launch the career of one of the greatest names of Brazilian music with the musical *Rosa de Ouro*. Clementina de Jesus was born in February 1901. She did not play to a large audience until the age of 63. Jesus had a long history in samba, having directed the samba schools Unidos do Riachuelo and Unidos do Engenho Velho, but for most of her life, she worked as a housekeeper.[53] Her double career as a domestic worker and a musician and the fact that she was a black woman who was only recognized for her talent later in life drove several comparisons between her and Lara. Together, they recorded the most beautiful rendition of "Sonho Meu." Lara would later pay homage to her friend with the song "Rainha Quelé" (Queen Quelé), which she wrote with Delcio Carvalho and incorporated into the album *A Arte do Encontro* (1986), with Jovelina Pérola Negra. Quelé was Clementina de Jesus's childhood nickname.

Besides his success as a producer and musical director, Bello de Carvalho was a songwriter. Born in 1935, he was a prolific writer and poet and is now one of the most respected experts in Brazilian music. The song "Unhas" (Nails) was recorded by another renowned singer before being shortlisted for *Sorriso Negro*. In 1979, Elizeth Cardoso included it on the album *O inverno do meu tempo* (The Winter of My Time), in a version that leaves nothing to be desired even to the purest of samba admirers. The harmonic progression dialogues with the lyrics, underlining the evolving cruelty of a lover who sticks fingernails into the heart of the interpreter, to later "rip, skin, kill" it. The lyrics of "Unhas," however, were a reason for a bad review of *Sorriso Negro*. She sings that the loved one behaves like a hawk, "*Que quando pica um coração / É pra esganá-lo de amor*" (That when stings a heart / Wants to strangle it with love). Critic José Ramos Tinhorão complained: "well, as everyone knows, to strangle is to kill by suffocation. Apparently, suffocating a heart with the beak, not even João do Vale's Carcará could."[54]

In *Sorriso Negro*, the nylon acoustic guitar carries "Unhas" with a counterpoint of the electric bass. The traditional instruments of samba (*surdo*, tambourines, *tantã*, and *pandeiro*) follow the main melody. As soon as Lara starts to sing, there are two dissonant chords. Throughout the song, there is a soft drum set, a cheerful wood block, and a prominent bass line. When the *cuíca* joins the drums, it feels like a typical samba from Rio de Janeiro. Interestingly, however, the traditional *partido-alto* mood sounds more inventive, with a groovy arrangement in the later part of the song, when Lara sings "*Você, ah, você*" (You, oh, you). She then invites the *tantã* to join her, when playing around with the melody and saying, "*Vai, tan tan tan*" (Go, tan tan tan), which can be interpreted as either her mimicking the sound of the drums or calling the instrument by its name.

Hermínio Bello de Carvalho recalls that he had known Lara for years before they became musical partners. Her melodies had always attracted him. Unlike what happened in most of her collaborations with Delcio de Carvalho, in "Unhas" Bello de Carvalho showed her the lyrics, and she later added the music. They only composed two songs together. The other one, "Mas quem disse que eu te esqueço" (an informal way of saying "But I Still Cannot Forget You") is one of Lara's biggest successes. Zeca Pagodinho, Mart'nália, Beth Carvalho, Áurea Martins, and many others have recorded versions of it. The lyrics hold a similar "love hurts" feeling, suggesting that even if someone were putting a knife in its chest, the singer would never forget the loved one ("*Puseram a faca em meu peito / Mas quem disse que eu te esqueço*").

The same composition process happened in both songs: Bello de Carvalho wrote the lyrics first, showed it to Lara, and waited for her melody.

I remember that with "Mas quem disse que eu te esqueço" we were in Brasília, doing a project together, project Pixinguinha, I think. I was sharing a room with Sidney Miller. We were writing, talking when Dona Ivone Lara passed by us. I had planned to send the poem to Sérgio Ricardo, but I showed it to her, and she jumped on it saying she would write the music.[55]

Months later, Lara called him with the news. "'Hey, partner,' she said, 'the song is ready, but I have to tell you, it was too long, so I got rid of some parts.' I told her to do whatever she wanted, of course. It was such a joy to have her writing another song with me."[56]

Tendência

Jorge Aragão does not remember the process of composing "Tendência." On a TV show broadcast in 2011 at TV Brasil, he said that Dona Ivone Lara once sang him an astonishing song. "This is Dona Ivone Lara," he exclaimed. Then she looked at him, expecting him to say something. He did not, and she asked: "Do you know whose song is this?" "Isn't it yours?" he replied. "Ah, ok. So, I guess I will take it all for me. This samba is yours, too, can't you remember? We wrote it together in Santos." Jorge Aragão laughed, and Lara joked that if she had wanted to, she could have stolen it.[57] The confusion, even for the coauthor, is understandable. "Tendência" follows the sophisticated and romantic melodies that became Lara's trademark.

Since Aragão does not remember having composed it, Pretinho da Serrinha, who is deeply familiar with the work of both artists, guesses as to its origin: "The chorus is 100% Dona Ivone Lara. It is her melody, for sure. Maybe he did the lyrics, but the melody, I am sure is not his, because his melodies are not like that, with everything so connected. Except for the beginning of the song, when there are those grave notes . . . that is probably Aragão."[58]

Born in 1949 in the suburban area of Padre Miguel, in Rio de Janeiro, Jorge Aragão da Cruz became known in 1976, when

Elza Soares recorded "Malandro," which Aragão composed with João Batista Alcantâra almost a decade earlier. Alcantâra, known as Jotabê, was the one to introduce Aragão to the samba world. Aragão has always been a discreet yet active figure. He was one of the founders of Cacique de Ramos and Grupo Fundo de Quintal. In *De Pé no chão* (1978), Beth Carvalho recorded "Vou Festejar," (I'll Celebrate) by Aragão, Edel Ferreira de Lima (Dida), and Neoci Dias de Andrade. The label Ariola released his first solo album, *Jorge Aragão*, in 1981.[59]

His importance to samba, however, started long before that. It is nearly impossible to describe how transformative were the meetings between Aragão and his partners in Olaria, in the suburbs of Rio de Janeiro. As described in the first part of this book, his group Fundo de Quintal brought samba back to the mainstream media and music market in the late 1970s. More than that, they reinvented Brazilian music, hosting musical reunions, creating new instruments, and reshaping the rhythm. Initially, the group was formed by Aragão, Sombrinha, Sereno (who invented the musical instrument *tantã*), Ubirany (creator of the *repique-de-mão*), Almir Guineto (one of the greatest sambistas of all times, who played a hybrid instrument: a banjo with the neck of a *cavaquinho*), Noeci (son of the revered samba composer João da Baiana), and Bira Presidente. "It was a revolution for Brazilian music. At that point, radios privileged foreign music, and we broke with that. Samba revitalized. Dona Ivone Lara, Beth Carvalho, Zeca Pagodinho, you name it. They were all closely connected to Fundo de Quintal," acknowledges Bira Presidente.[60]

Fundo de Quintal became a central influence in Lara's work, and *Sorriso Negro* is the album that best represents that. "I can't even remember if we played in the recording of the album *Sorriso Negro* because we did practically everything together. So, I would say, yes. I do know that we played at the concert. Actually, we played with Dona Ivone Lara for decades, we traveled the world together, either as her guests or inviting her to play with us," recalls Bira.[61]

The influence of Fundo de Quintal in *Sorriso Negro*'s recording of "Tendência" is clear. Led by the tambourines, several traditional samba instruments permeate the background, with a complete "*cozinha*," which translates literally to "kitchen," meaning the entire team of samba percussive instruments. However, the beautiful and sophisticated melody—a quality of Jorge Aragão and Dona Ivone Lara compositions—goes beyond the traditional samba. Flutes with a chromatic pattern add a jazz or bossa nova flair. Sometimes the *cavaquinho* conducts the melodic line and the counterpoints. At other times, Hélvius Vilela's piano does. Vilela (1941–2010) became known as a jazz and bossa nova composer and player. From 1964 to 1967, he was a member of Tempo Trio. He also worked with Milton Nascimento, Carlos Lyra, Edu Lobo, Elizeth Cardoso, Quarteto em Cy, and more frequently, with Rosinha de Valença. In *Sorriso Negro*, he conducts two songs: "Me Deixa Ficar" and "Alguém Me Avisou." All the other songs in the album, including "Tendência," are conducted and arranged by Rosinha de Valença. "Tendência," however, is the one in which the elements of samba and bossa nova more clearly intertwine.

By the end of the song, the *cavaquinho* occupies a more frontal position, with the flute counterpointing with Lara's voice. There is a freedom that almost feels like a jazz improvisation. There are moments when the song sounds like a typical *partido-alto*, with a loud and imposing *cavaquinho*. At other times, the strong piano suggests some tension. The lyrics set the terrain for a broken heart and complains about the terrible behavior of the loved one. First, in the chorus the singer says that the loved one invaded her life only to use and abuse her, doing whatever was convenient. Then, she refers to cruelty: "*Não me comove o pranto de quem é ruim*" (I do not feel for the tears of those who are bad). In the end, however, when the tension between the *cavaquinho* and the piano is resolved, the lyrics follow the harmonic love story to indicate forgiveness: "*Se precisar pode me procurar*" (If you need, you can look for me—an expression that roughly corresponds to "I'll be there for you"). After the tag, the seven-string guitar does the outro alone, closing the musical dialogue.

The lyrics of "Tendência," about a sad yet hopeful love story, can lead those unfamiliar with Aragão's work to think he writes romantic songs. He does, but this is only a small part of his prolific career. In 1986, a few years after the recording of "Tendência," Aragão composed one of his most successful sambas, "Coisa de Pele" (Skin Thing), in which he praises black heritage, proclaiming that it was about time that black Brazilians embraced their race. He also states that "*Foi bom insistir, compor e ouvir / Resiste quem pode à força dos nossos pagodes*" (It was good to insist, compose and listen / Only few can resist to the strength of our *pagodes*). Influenced by the Black Movement, he wrote several other songs about racism in Brazil, including the assertive "Identidade" (1992), in which he criticizes a symbol of Brazilian racial oppression: the freight elevator. He demands that Brazilian society refuse to use it.[62] He also states that a black person with a white soul should never be perceived as an example of dignity. "*Quem cede a vez não quer vitória / Somos herança da memória*" (Who gives its turn does not want to win / We are a heritage of our memory). At the time of *Sorriso Negro*, these discussions were ebullient.

Part 3

Sorriso Negro

A person unfamiliar with the history of the Catholic church known as Irmandade Nossa Senhora do Rosário dos Pretos, in Salvador, Bahia, would undoubtedly be astonished by the drums and lyrics of its religious hymns. Though one might expect messages of redemption in God's hands, here they talk about black identity, respect, and pride. A famous song of praise, included in the masses every week since it became famous in the voice of Dona Ivone Lara, describes the power of a black smile and how it is capable of bringing joy to everyone around. The song also suggests that a black person without a job becomes restless, and it proclaims: "*Negro é a raiz da liberdade*" (Black is the root of freedom). In the lyrics, the Portuguese word "negro" refers sometimes to a black person, at others to an entire racial category, and at times to the color black. The song is "Sorriso Negro," by Adilson Barbado, Jorge Portela, and Jair do Cavaco, immortalized by Lara.[1] The composers list several reasons why being black should be a reason to feel pride.

The Irmandade Nossa Senhora do Rosário dos Pretos was founded in 1685 and officially recognized as a Third Order in 1899.[2] It is one of the most visited churches of the neighborhood of Pelourinho, named a world heritage site by the United Nations Educational, Scientific, and Cultural Organization (UNESCO).[3] However, it is not a regular Catholic house of worship. Instead of conventional ceremonies, it celebrates Catholic masses with Afro-Brazilian music and dance.[4] It is a strong and traditional black lay brotherhood (*irmandade negra*)—a community built around one patron saint. These institutions played a crucial role in seventeenth-century Brazil.[5]

The *irmandade negra* allowed for a high degree of syncretism, embracing African-Brazilian religions and Christianity and welcoming enslaved people from different areas of Africa— but in the case of Nossa Senhora do Rosário dos Pretos, mostly from Congo and Angola.[6] They became organized spaces on which these black communities could rely for help in practical situations of daily life, from health issues to language difficulties. They were also places where debates on identity prevailed and played an instrumental role in the development of black consciousness during the colonial regime. João José Reis writes that

> their value as instruments of resistance is indisputable. They allowed the construction or reformulation of identities that functioned as a bulkhead to the disintegration of collectivities subject to immense pressures. Even if they have been selective in the alliances promoted, they have shown, in many cases, that it is possible to coexist despite differences, without prejudice against the ability to resist. Its biggest limit, of course, was slavery itself, which was not accepted without criticism.[7]

In a time of crisis for Catholicism in the racially mixed capital of Brazil, black lay brotherhoods also played a role in strengthening Christianity. They contributed to the affirmation of the sacraments of the church and to preserve the worship of the saints.[8]

Salvador was the Brazilian capital for over two centuries, from 1549 and 1763. As the main port for slave traffic, the city became a melting pot of African, European, and Amerindian cultures. Although it is hard to pinpoint the exact number of enslaved Africans who arrived in Brazil via Bahia, the estimates are over 1.3 million.[9] However, the city was destined to be more than just the center of the slave trade and international exchange. It was also a center of domestic commerce. The area known as Recôncavo has a geography that allowed connections with neighborhoods of Salvador that were linked to areas of sugar production in the Northeast, thus creating a vibrant network between urban and rural Brazil. At this rich crossroads, African music and dances flourished.[10]

The fact that "Sorriso Negro" is part of the liturgy and celebrations of Nossa Senhora do Rosário dos Pretos is a testament to what a vigorous symbol it is for the Afro-Brazilian community. In mass, the song is played after the priest says, "The peace of the Lord be with you always," to which the community responds: "And with your spirit." Then, the priest instructs the congregation to "offer each other the sign of peace." In Brazilian Catholic churches, it is common for people to hug and kiss at this moment. At Nossa Senhora do Rosário dos Pretos, this is when the song "Sorriso Negro" starts to play. While greeting other members of the church, they sing the lyrics slowly, clapping at the rhythm of the African drums that compose the church's band. In the album *Rosário dos Pretos—Cânticos* (1999), Lara recorded the song with Ilê Aiyê, a group founded in 1974 in Salvador that developed as a renowned *bloco-Afro*, a carnival group that features themes of black culture and promotes the beauty of blackness.[11]

It is no coincidence that Dona Ivone Lara decided to include the song—which she did not write—on *Sorriso Negro* and name the album after it. The lyrics state that blacks are beautiful, inspiring, and should be respected. They also contend that slavery, silence, and mourning are part of black identity. At times the lyrics may even seem too simple and straightforward. The opening verses declare that a black smile or hug has the power to bring happiness to the world, and that *"Negro sem emprego, fica sem sossego"* (A black person without a job becomes unrested). The clarity of the lyrics, however, should be interpreted as urgency, for it carries the essential aspirations of the Black Movement in Brazil: social equality, respect, and an end to racism. Singer Juliana Ribeiro contends that when one sings of one's own history, there is a level of appropriation that cannot be matched. "When Dona Ivone Lara sings 'Sonho Meu,' well, it is a love story, something that anyone can identify with. But when she states that black is beautiful, sings her own history, she takes the lyrics to a different place, one that can only be achieved from someone within a locus of enunciation that embraces the Afro-Brazilian music, culture, and experience."[12]

Philosopher, activist, and theatrologist Thereza Santos engaged in a powerful quest for black identity inside the Brazilian Black Movement. She asserts that the myth of racial democracy coupled with the arbitrariness of racial designations in Brazil (in the census, these include "chocolate," "coffee and milk," "mulatto," and "cinnamon," among others) resulted in the detachment of the Afro-Brazilian population from black consciousness.[13] Santos argues that one of the central objectives of the Black Movement was to denounce the "genocide practiced against blacks in its different forms: the murders committed by the police; the subhuman conditions generated by the total lack of access to the most elementary conditions of survival; the sterilization of black women; the mental genocide practiced through the stigmas and prototypes that destroy blacks' self-esteem and dignity."[14]

I return, then, to the idea of *resistance by existence*. Dona Ivone Lara does not engage in political activism, although *Sorriso Negro* was—and still is—an instrument of the promotion of black power. She does not directly demand equality, although she influenced several women who came after her to engage in activities that had been until then considered to be exclusively male. The broad concept of intellectual activism, which Patricia Hill Collins defines as "the myriad ways that people place the power of their ideas in service to social justice," is hardly applicable to her case.[15] Lara does not talk about social justice. She is merely asserting her identity. Nevertheless, in doing so, she generates a considerable social impact. If, like Thereza Santos, Abdias do Nascimento, and so many other leaders of the Brazilian Black Movement have claimed, Afro-Brazilians suffered from the underdevelopment of racial consciousness, her biography addresses this absence. The memory of her achievements is a central part of the forging of the Brazilian black identity.

One smile for two

When writing about the song "Sorriso Negro," scholar Katia Santos compares Dona Ivone Lara to the figure of a *griot*, "a member of a class of traveling poets, musicians, and storytellers who maintain a tradition of oral history in parts of West Africa."[16] The parallel is justified by the fact that Lara embraces the mission of passing down through generations the sentiments of the Brazilian black community. Her decision not only to include the song but also to name the album after it demonstrates how unavoidable the need to express the feelings of black Brazilians was for her. Santos highlights the fact that the lyrics are almost naïve, but at the same time, they were a then necessary acknowledgment of the humanity of blacks.[17]

Adilson Barbado, one of the authors of the song, confesses that many people still think that Dona Ivone Lara wrote "Sorriso Negro."[18] The album cover only lists two of the composers, Adilson Barbado and Jorge Portela, an indication that even for Warner Music, the authorship was unclear. Leandro Braga explains that the misattribution to Lara makes sense. "It is the name of the album, it became popular after her rendition, and it has some characteristics common with her work: the first part is more floating, with long notes, above the rhythmic syncopation, while the second part is more agitated, with shorter notes. And there are also the 'jumps' in both parts."[19] Barbado comments that the confusion does not bother him because, although the song was not composed for Lara, it belongs to her voice.

Not only to hers but also to Jorge Ben Jor's, at the time still using the name Jorge Ben. Jorge Duilio Lima Menezes was born in Rio de Janeiro in 1942 to a mother of Ethiopian descent and a father described as an "European melting pot."[20] In the 1960s, he played at Beco das Garrafas, where several prominent musicians of bossa nova became known, including Rosinha de Valença. Jorge Ben, however, did not play bossa nova. He also claims that he is not a sambista, although he acknowledges that he can write "pretty good sambas."[21] His music has been described as samba rock, funk, samba esquema novo (a kind of modern version of samba which was also the name of his 1963 album), and so many other classifications it would be fairer to simply state that his is a distinctive musical style, one that embodies a little bit of everything. Researcher Luiz Tatit summarized the 1970s as a time when Brazilian music set itself free from "predefined rhythmic genres."[22]

It was the age of Tropicalism, the movement that arose in the late 1960s led by some of the greatest names of Brazilian music, such as Os Mutantes, Tom Zé, Caetano Veloso, Gilberto Gil, Gal Costa, and Torquato Neto.[23] They embodied the principles of the *Anthropophagic Manifesto*, published in 1928 by the Brazilian poet Oswald de Andrade, which defended that Brazil's greatest strength was a kind of cultural cannibalism, the embracing of different influences that created something unique. Tropicalistas flirted with rock, samba, theater, poetry. Although he is a contemporary of the movement, Jorge Ben is considered a central influence to it precisely because of his pioneering mix of different musical and literary references.

At the time of *Sorriso Negro*, Jorge Ben had already released some of his most notable works, including *A Tábua de Esmeralda* (1974), *Solta o Pavão* (1975), and *África Brasil* (1976).[24] One of Ben's best-known works, *África Brasil*, deeply explores Afro-Brazilian and African American music styles. For the first time in an album, he replaced the acoustic guitar with the electric guitar in all tracks. However, as in previous works, percussive instruments were front and center. Timbales, *surdo*, congas, and *cuíca* create a funkiness that at that point was unprecedented.[25] Most of the lyrics were directly connected to Africa. The first song, for example, "Ponta de lança africano (Umbabarauma)," is about an African soccer player. Also on this album is the story of Xica da Silva, a Brazilian-born slave who became rich and powerful.[26] Zumbi dos Palmares—a quilombola who led the maroon community Quilombo dos Palmares and fought against slavery in Brazil—is at the center of "Africa Brasil (Zumbi)," in which Ben asks *"Eu quero ver o que vai acontecer quando Zumbi chegar"* (I want to see what will happen when Zumbi arrives).[27]

The multiplicity of references present in Ben's music is also evident in his and Lara's rendition of "Sorriso Negro." The Afro-Brazilianess of the song meets, right at the beginning, a beautiful fingerpicking pattern on the seven-string acoustic guitar. The percussive instruments create different colors of sound as they are played with a stick. Suddenly, a concertina invades the ensemble. The traditional samba is there, with the *surdo* doing the samba call and the *cuíca* screaming back, like a suffering soul. Tambourines, cavaquinho, guitar, bass, full samba percussions—all the typical instruments of the rhythm are there. Lara and Ben sing a call-and-answer to which the concertina sometimes does the counterpoint. They do it as if they were truly smiling throughout the song. At one point, Ben proclaims: "*Dona Ivone Lara no terreiro*," a reference to the meeting place for African-Brazilian cults. She later improvises "*Ai, São Jorge, vai chover na minha horta*" (literally, "Ah, St. George, it will rain in my garden," an idiomatic expression in Portuguese which is equivalent to being on a roll or having a streak of good luck). The joke refers to Saint George, Jorge Ben's namesake in Portuguese and also one of the most symbolically important saints of Brazilian syncretism. He is linked to Ogum, the god of the war in African-Brazilian religions Candomblé and Umbanda. The song ends with all singing together and a final chord that is not very typical of the traditional samba; it nods to bossa nova, with sevenths and ninths.

Initially, though, the song was thought to be a traditional samba. Adilson Barbado recalls that he, Jorge Portela, and Jair de Carvalho wrote the song little by little, in roughly one month, in the late 1970s. He does not remember the exact date but recalls that the cultural environment at the time—one of questioning racism and racial inequality—was the main source of inspiration. "The idea was to show how much black people worked, all the challenges they confronted, and how they were happy despite all that."[28] The notion that happiness in the face of adversity is a good thing, however, is a contentious one. In the United States, many viewed Louis Armstrong smiling demeanor as a sign of compliance.[29] In Brazil, contemporary rap groups, such as Racionais MCs, embraced activism and rejected any suggestion of subservience.[30] I could not find, however, traces of criticism along these lines to this particular idea of "Sorriso Negro" in 1980s Brazil. The smile was perceived more as a celebration of the beauty of blackness than as a sign of deference.

At the time they composed the song, Barbado worked at Rio de Janeiro Stock Exchange, while Jorge Portela and Jair de Carvalho were retired. Barbado recalls that they sang "Sorriso Negro" in a *roda de samba*; Lara heard it and asked for the tape. "Some people knew the lyrics in the samba scene, but it was when she recorded it that it became a huge success. I think it was due to her voice. She is the song. She is black."[31] For him, the name of the album was what turned it into a unique symbol of the fight against racism in Brazil.

In a 2008 interview with the Museum of Sound and Image of Rio de Janeiro, Lara recollects it differently. She said the song was brought to her by a relative of her husband who arrived at her house "with a *cavaquinho* with three strings [laughs]. But he was all full of himself. A great songwriter. Actually, he was a great songwriter. He said: you are recording an album, so listen to this song, 'Sorriso Negro,' which I wrote. I want you to record it."[32] She said, however, that it was a "totally different 'Sorriso Negro.' I thought it was really weird; he spoke about so many things. So, I told him, 'You see, I don't like politics, so you won't be bothered if I include one little thing here or there, right? I don't want a collaboration; I don't need you to put my name or anything.'"[33]

According to Lara's testimony, she sang the song for the first time in São Paulo at a May 13th celebration, when Brazilians remember the abolishment of slavery. Lara claims it was an instant success only due to her intervention, but asserts that "the song is mine, but the lyrics are his, but it is completely different. Until this day, when people say "'Sorriso Negro,' by Dona Ivone Lara,' I state 'Sorriso Negro' is not mine. I have my other collaborations."[34]

Lara also rejects the idea that her music should be used to educate or engage the audience, as the composer and politician Leci Brandão does. In an interview, she declared: "I do not let go of any opportunity of denouncing racism. I'll go to the podium, and I'll tell you. When I see black girls, they say, 'You represent me.'"[35] Despite that, Brandão defends that Lara's existence, attitude, and success engage with a narrative of the feminist and Black Movement in Brazil. For singer Mart'nália, the song symbolizes the truth of what blackness is: "It is a way of unifying blacks and whites through samba, practically forcing everyone to sing that black is beautiful."[36] She contends that the supposed simplicity and naivety of the lyrics are an instrument of engagement. "There is no way a white person will sing that a black smile doesn't bring joy," she laughs. "It is very straightforward, very political. It is almost like a hoax. While singing it, the person is affirming that we, blacks, are the gear of the entire thing, that samba is black, is female."[37] Pretinho da Serrinha, whose nickname means "little black," admits he sings the song as a political statement. "It is a beautiful samba but more than that, it is an assertion. To say that black is a color one should respect will never be naïve. It is a bold, strong affirmation. It is to teach a lesson, to state that *black is the root of freedom*."[38]

Samba and dictatorship

In the mid-1970s, Lara, Clementina de Jesus, and other *sambistas* presented what the TV show *Fantástico* called "a protest of *sambistas* against the invasion of soul music." They chose not to embrace the ideas of Pan-Africanism or the US Civil Rights Movement, engaging instead in a repudiation of this musical genre.[39] As Steve Bocskay states, in "Sou Mais o Samba" (something close to "I prefer samba"), "Candeia, Dona Ivone Lara, and Clementina de Jesus, along with numerous *sambistas*, dancers, and common folk declare with pride not their Afro-Brazilian identity but their Brazilian national identity."[40] Lara appears on the show playing a "*prato-e-faca*," literally a dish and a knife, and singing verses that explicitly declare a refusal to self-identify as African or North American.

In the late 1960s, when Lara became a constant presence of Rio de Janeiro's samba scene, the distinctive rhythm had long been one of the major symbols of Brazilian culture. The military regime coincided with a second golden age for samba, a period when, besides her, Martinho da Vila, Zé Keti, Paulinho da Viola, and many others became mainstream. Samba reaffirmed itself as the primary representation of Brazilianess, in opposition to soul and black music. It was—and still is—a central part of Brazilian identity. During the dictatorship, this quality was exploited politically. In the soccer World Cup of 1970, at the height of the violence of the dictatorship, samba composer Miguel Gustavo wrote the *marcha* "Pra Frente Brasil" (Onwards, Brazil), calling for the union of the entire nation to push the Brazil squad. It became the theme song of the regime.

"Sou Mais o Samba" ended up coinciding with the views of the dictatorship, embracing samba but refusing to engage in debates about race. For the National Security Council of Brazil, documenting or suggesting the existence of racism in Brazil was in itself an act of subversion. Several scholars who discussed the topic ended up being forcefully retired from their academic positions.[41] The rise of soul music in Rio de Janeiro became part of a national discussion about what should qualify as confrontational to the regime. Paulina Alberto recalls an article published by *Jornal do Brasil* in which journalist Lena Frias coined the term "Black Rio."[42] Frias referred to an "imported" pride to be black, a reference to the civil rights movement.[43] Alberto contends that the dance craze in Brazil brought debates about racial terminology, identity, and the real extent of racism prevalent in the country, which at this point seemed closer to the United States than part of the Brazilian society wanted to admit.[44] The soul music parties also confused the police. The officers believed that foreigners, especially North Americans, were driving the movement. They assumed it was impossible for Brazilians to have developed such ideas.[45]

Lara became an emblem of Brazilianess—of what was seen to be genuinely, originally Brazilian. Antônio Candeia Filho and Manacéia led the movement to preserve the "real samba" with a particular attachment to *partido-alto*. "*Partido-alto*, I have said before, is the most authentic expression of samba," affirmed Candeia in the first scene of Leon Hirszman's 1982 documentary *Partido Alto,* which captured the samba scene in the mid-1970s. However, this crusade to preserve Brazilian tradition, which seduced even leftists, was not wholly removed from the idea that samba and blackness walked side by side. Dmitri Cerboncini Fernandes claims that the influence of the civil rights movement and the embrace of black identity in Brazil actually enhanced the vision of samba as not only a national symbol but also a mark of Afro-Brazilian traditions.[46] He cites as an example the founding, in 1975, of the Grêmio Recreativo de Arte Negra Escola de Samba Quilombo, a movement that several *sambistas* joined, including Candeia, Paulinho da Viola, and Elton Medeiros. Fernandes and Bocskay's competing views demonstrate the complexity of the position of these musicians during a time when there were heightened tensions between race and nationalism. The call to reject US racial terminology as well as to acknowledge the virulent racism in Brazil complicated the expansion of the Black Movement.[47]

Although the dictatorship did not persecute or force into exile as many *sambistas* as it did artists of other genres, the group was not free from oppression. Samba schools changed to resist.[48] In 1969, for the first carnival after Institutional Act Number Five, Silas de Oliveira composed with Mano Décio da Viola and Manuel Ferreira the official *samba-enredo* of Império Serrano. "Heróis da Liberdade" was about the Inconfidência Mineira.[49] The composers were made to alter one verse because it was considered to be a criticism of the regime.[50] The song narrated a situation in which, while listening to the sound of soldiers and drums from afar, students and teachers sang that freedom had arrived. It spoke of the flame that hatred could not extinguish "*É a revolução em sua legítima razão*" (literally, "It is the revolution in its rightful reason," meaning that it was a rightful revolution), a verse that the composers had to modify to "*É a evolução em sua legítima razão*" (It is the evolution in its rightful reason, which can refer to evolution in general, or to the samba evolution, a category in the carnival competition in which the jurors evaluate the speed and the engagement of the components of the samba school in the parade.)

Silencing a movement

The rejection of international music was echoed in the discourses of nationalism that prevailed during the dictatorship. The transformation of samba into a national symbol has guided the work of several scholars. Anthropologist Hermano Vianna investigates the events that converted the rhythm from a statement of vagrancy into a source for Brazilian pride. Vianna recounts a meeting between a group of white men who represented the intelligentsia and erudite art world of Brazil in the 1930s—Gilberto Freyre, Sérgio Buarque de Holanda, Villa-Lobos, and Luciano Gallet—and a group of black musicians from the more impoverished areas of Rio de Janeiro: Pixinguinha, Donga, and Patrício Teixeira. Vianna also mentions the so-called "tendency toward sincerity, which made a Brazilian honest enough to recognize himself deeply affected by black influence."[51] There was also a kind of national spirit, driven by a will to promote unity. Politician Afonso Arinos, who wrote the first legislation against racism in Brazil in the early 1950s, summarized this search for a national symbol as a necessity in a broken nation.[52] Arinos claimed that "Brazil is so regionalized that for the provinces not to be absolutely strange to each other, it takes a great effort to fortify the moral unity of the country."[53]

The publication of Gilberto Freyre's *The Masters and the Slaves* in the early 1930s provoked a commotion—and continues to be at the center of the work of scholars of Brazil. In 1946, at the time of its first printing in English translation in the United States, critics called it "the best book ever written on Brazil."[54] Although at this point he had not coined the expression "racial democracy," Freyre's work contributed to the acceptance of the idea that Brazil was a country free of racism. His central argument was that miscegenation, endorsed and accepted, was directly connected to state formation, identity, and religion. The anthropologist described the Jesuit system as "possibly the most efficient force for technical Europeanization and intellectual and moral culture in its effect upon the natives."[55] What Freyre came to call "Lusotropicalism"—the Portuguese promotion of miscegenation—was central to the formation of the Brazilian state. Iberians, he claimed, allowed greater autonomy to the black population, inviting them to integrate into Brazilian society easily. The legal system was more condescending to blacks, and manumission was frequent. Freyre's point was that miscegenation was not the cause of terrible "eugenic" damage but, on the contrary, the creator of a "superior" society. The idea that the intense racial mixture could explain Brazilian "backwardness" began to be substituted by another myth: that the country was free of racism.[56]

Emília Viotti da Costa affirms that Freyre was not the only one to blame for this illusion. The notion of a raceless country had accompanied Brazil for centuries. For Viotti da Costa, the forging of Brazilian national identity was part of an elite project in which subaltern groups played a minimal role, and landowners ruled. She suggests that the enslaved population had some degree of agency, but a discreet one.[57] According to her, the tardiness of the abolition of slavery in Brazil was also related to the belief in racial democracy. When abolition did come, it was due to economic reasons, such as changes in market relations, exports production, and mechanization, which demanded a broader consumer market and a more efficient labor structure.

For Sérgio Buarque de Holanda, Brazilians are a "cordial" people who explore a form of negotiation based on the rejection of confrontation.[58] It is a way of interacting that is subtle and friendly, and this pretending does achieve some results. Florestan Fernandes refers to the use of racial democracy to hide racism as "the prejudice of having no prejudices." He argues that, by assuming and reinforcing the absence of racism, the state and Brazilian society fail to fight it. The myth of racial democracy is fundamentally an elite strategy to preserve its privileges by silencing social conflicts.[59]

The Brazilian Black Movement was not a simple amalgamation of ideas that grew with other black movements around the world, especially in the United States. One can argue that the influence was mutual. The civil rights movement of the 1950s and 1960s served as a model for Brazilians who would create institutions with similar objectives in the 1970s. However, many contemporary organizations were still influenced by the circulation of the ideas of the Black Atlantic.[60] The Frente Negra Brasileira (FNB), for instance, was an essential reference for the civil rights movement since the 1930s.[61]

The Black Movement of the 1970s

The origins of the Black Movement in Brazil can be traced back to the *quilombos*, groups of runaway enslaved people who resisted the oppression of the government, which had the most substantial slave trade in the Western Hemisphere. Others claim that it only became an organized movement with the founding, in 1931, of the FNB and the Black Experimental Theater in the 1940s. However, during the dictatorship (1964–1985), denouncing racism could result in being charged with subversion, and the movement grew weak and disorganized.[62] Only in the late 1970s, with the *Abertura* and the authorization for all the remaining exiles to return home, did these institutions bloom again. Following the influence of the civil rights movement and the increasing willingness to question the myth of racial democracy, the Black Movement in Brazil brought an agenda that centered on the pride of being a black Brazilian and the rejection of whitening as a form of social inclusion.[63]

In 1978, a series of events made the denial of racism in Brazil unsustainable. In April, police officers from São Paulo tortured and killed a 27-year-old worker, Robson Silveira da Luz. He was accused of stealing fruits from a street market, a narrative that resembled racial crimes in the United States. In May, in another episode of acute racism, four black boys were dismissed from the Tiete Yacht Club. Although the major newspapers of the time did not give much space to these events, the Marxist publication *Versus* dedicated broad coverage to them.[64] In response, the Unified Movement Against Racial Discrimination (MUCDR) made its first sizable public appearance, leading a demonstration in São Paulo. In July of that same year, more than 2,000 people reunited to listen to speakers and protest against racism in Brazil.[65]

The MUCDR would soon become the Unified Black Movement, *Movimento Negro Unificado* (MNU). Lélia Gonzáles, together with one of the founders of the Black Experimental Theater, Abdias do Nascimento, decided that "against racial discrimination" could become the motto; the name of the group, however, must focus on blacks.[66] Little by little, MNU became a large institution. A series of National Assemblies took place in several states, gathering activists from Rio de Janeiro, Bahia, São Paulo, Minas Gerais, and Espírito Santo. The movement created small organizations called *centros de luta* (CL), which consisted of "a minimum of five persons who accepted the statutes and the program of the MNU and would promote debates, information, consciousness raising and the organization of Black people."[67] The centers acted wherever they could find blacks, including in work areas and *candomblé* temples. By the late 1970s, the movement was stronger than ever, with protests and conferences happening almost every week. In October 1979, MNU organized a symbolic burial of the Afonso Arinos Law, which forbade racial discrimination in Brazil.[68]

The strength of MNU was part of a broader change in Brazilian society. Although the development of "Black Rio" cannot be considered an organized political movement, it raised a new level of racial consciousness that had broad impact on fashion, dance, and, certainly, Brazilian music.[69] The arts became central to affirming black racial pride. In 1976, Milton Nascimento released the single "Raça," which opened the album *Milton*.

The verses mention several icons of Afro-Brazilian culture, including actor Grande Otelo, samba composer Monsueto, and singer Clementina de Jesus. Nascimento defines blackness, among other things, as "*É Clementina cantando bonito / As aventuras do seu povo aflito*" (It is Clementina singing beautifully / The adventures of her afflicted people).

In 1982, almost in parallel with *Sorriso Negro*, came Sandra de Sá's recording of "Olhos Coloridos" by Jards Macalé, in which a proud Afro-Brazilian sings that "*A verdade é que você (e todo brasileiro) / Tem sangue crioulo*" (The truth is that you [and all Brazilians] / Have black blood). Jorge Aragão—who coauthored "Tendência" with Dona Ivone Lara—recorded, in 1986, "Coisa de Pele," a song in which he proposes thinking of maroon community Quilombo dos Palmares. He invites the audience to finally break the ties with the past and with international influence, understanding that good things also came from the inside. He invited the listener to smile because nothing could prevent one from doing so. And stated that one cannot get away from this "skin thing." *Sorriso Negro* was born in this moment of contestation and consciousness. It embodies these questions; soon, it would become a symbol of the reshaping of black identity in Brazil.

Axé de langa

Another part of this broader transformation can be seen in "Axé de langa," the last song on *Sorriso Negro*. Full of references to Candomblé, *jongo*, and to African heritage, the song was composed at a time when Dona Ivone Lara's memory of

Africa was more intense than ever. In 1980, she joined over sixty people who, led by Brazilian singer and songwriter Chico Buarque and producer Fernando Faro, traveled to Angola to perform in the May 1st festivities, which mark Workers Day in both countries. The invitation came from Agostinho Neto, who served as the first president of Angola from 1975 to 1979 and led the Popular Movement for the Liberation of Angola (MPLA) in the war of independence and the civil war. He was also the country's preeminent poet. The tour was named "Project Kalunga," a Bantu word that refers to a deity related to death, the sea, and Hell. Kalunga is present in the folklore of each of the two nations.[70] The newspaper *O Globo* called the tour the "largest musical-artistic Brazilian caravan to have ever performed internationally."[71] Besides Dona Ivone Lara, other acclaimed names of Brazilian music boarded the TAAG (Angolan Aerial Transports) Boeing 707 to Luanda, among them, Dorival Caymmi, Martinho da Vila, Djavan, Elba Ramalho, Wanda Sá, Geraldo Azevedo, Clara Nunes, Edu Lobo, João do Vale, João Nogueira, and Miucha. Lara was in one of the front seats, near Francis Hime, Olivia Hime, filmmaker Ruy Guerra, and Chico Buarque and his family. It was what singer Djavan called "the living room."[72]

At this point, Brazil and Angola shared not only a language and a colonial past but also contemporary cultural manifestations. The Brazilian *telenovelas O Bem Amado* and *Gabriela* were big hits in the African country. Brazilian music could be heard in the streets. Dulcy Tupi, who wrote a detailed diary of the trip, recalls that the group visited beer and textile factories, the Museum of Independence, and the Museum of Anthropology.[73] They lamented not being able to go to the Museum of Slavery, which was under renovation. Tupi also points to several similarities between the sister countries. One day, the boat that had taken the artists for a ride broke down mid-trip, and many of the passengers took it as an opportunity to enjoy themselves, jumping in the ocean: "Another boat towed the boat back to the dock, where some soldiers unloaded another boat. We returned to the island. A mixed choir of Brazilians and Angolans sang 'Saudosa Maloca,' by Adoniran Barbosa, and 'Sei que é Covardia,' by Ataulfo Alves." Lara was the last on stage in the first concert, on May 10th. Martinho da Vila introduced her to the audience and, "with her harmonious whirls and spontaneous musicality, she received the most sincere applause."[74] The group performed in Benguela and Lobito before returning to Luanda. In the final concert, after Lara's presentation, all the artists went back on stage and sang her "Sonho Meu." Angolan songwriters Filipe Mukenga, Rui Mingas, and Waldemar Bastos also joined the group.[75]

"Axé de langa" almost transports the listener to Angola. *Jongo* is the major symbol of Serrinha, the neighborhood where Lara was raised.[76] The area proudly preserves the African tradition, which originated in Congo and Angola.[77] Bantu enslaved people brought the rhythm to Brazil, and it was disseminated in the area of the river Paraíba do Sul, along the states of Rio de Janeiro, São Paulo, and Minas Gerais. In the 1960s, Mestre Darcy decided to create a formal group, Jongo da Serrinha, to turn it into an organized cultural movement.[78] Some of the traditions of the music and dance disappeared in the name of preserving *jongo* through generations. For example, only a few decades ago children started participating in the *rodas*. During Lara's childhood, she would never have been allowed to be around a *jongo* celebration. The reason was that the traditional music has *pontos*—something similar to witchcraft but untranslatable into English—and practitioners feared they would not be able to make the spell vanish.[79] Fearing that *jongo* would disappear—it currently survives only in a few communities in the state of Rio de Janeiro— the elders decided to avoid the mystical words and allow anyone to enter the *roda*. Lara recalls that in her childhood she was limited to hearing the rhythm from afar, imagining that forbidden universe. She paid close attention to the accounts of those who used to accompany the ritual. Many said that the moment her Tia Tereza (aunt Tereza) entered the circle, everyone stopped to admire her.[80]

In the lyrics of "Axé de Ianga," Tia Tereza, who was Mestre Fuleiro's mother, is said to be the one who told stories about Lara's grandfather. The song describes how he would untie "brothers" and bathe them with *abô*, a mixture of plants and herbs used in several *Candomblé* rituals. The other woman mentioned in the lyrics is Vovó Maria (Grandma Maria), also known as Vovó Maria Joana, a *mãe-de-santo* and founder of the Tenda Espírita Cabana de Xangô, dedicated to the practice of the Afro-Brazilian religion Umbanda. She was also one of the founders of samba school Império Serrano. For Lara, *jongo* was a serious issue, not only because of the mysteries it embodied, but because of her own appreciation for traditions: "We had a fear of disrespecting that, you know? It was not just the fear of the worst, of the spell, but of disappointing the elders and ruining those customs that our ancestors had brought with them for so long."[81]

Also noticeable in the lyrics is the influence of Bantu dialects present in Angola and Congo. For Nei Lopes, *jongo* is part of a "black musical tradition" of Rio de Janeiro, a result of the migratory flows of the enslaved populations of coffee and sugar plantations.[82] Kazadi Wa Mukuna draws a parallel between *jongo* and samba, claiming that the former is an older version of the latter.[83] Singer Mat'nália highlights that this song is not about the melody but the drums. "It is a kind of religious mantra," she says, an affirmation of Sodré's idea of the prevalence of drums as a form of resistance.[84] Pretinho da Serrinha agrees that the simplicity of the song is typical in any *jongo*, with a chorus easy to memorize, which should be sung in unison by all participants in the *roda*. "For us, from Serrinha, *jongo* is a movement of cultural resistance. It became far more open to change as a strategy of survival."[85]

It is unavoidable, then, to see a resemblance to Lara's life in the most recent history of *jongo* and its quest to adapt so that it might survive. Uniquely, she represented a "truly Brazilian" individual who connects Africa, Europe, and indigenous cultures. She studied classical music with Lucília Villa-Lobos but adopted the *cavaquinho* (tuned as a mandolin) as her primary instrument. She became an icon of popular and Afro-Brazilian traditions by using tools derived from European erudite music. Lara was a black woman whose great-grandmother was a slave. She held within herself this Brazilian blurring of borders between body and mind, sacred and secular, soft and radical.

Afterword

Dona Ivone Lara died on April 16, 2018. It was an unusually cold Tuesday in New York. The day before, a good friend had texted me from Rio de Janeiro to let me know that she was in the hospital and refusing to eat. It was not typical of her to give up on anything, so I understood that she was, once again, doing things "because she wanted to." I woke up the following morning to see several messages from friends letting me know of her passing. I was in the final phase of editing this book, a couple of weeks before the deadline to send the manuscript to the editor. I spent the day giving interviews and talking about Dona Ivone Lara. In all of them, I tried to make sure she would not be remembered as an unfortunate victim of Brazilian society. For me, the inclination to reduce her to that is just a testament to the fact that we are still not ready for the majesty of her life. Lara was the leading actor of her biography, not allowing destiny to be in charge—unless she somehow wanted it to be.

Lara was one of the greatest stars of Brazilian music. "Dona," in Portuguese, can be translated as both "lady" and "owner," a title she embraced with talent and audacity, but also with a resilience that allowed her to navigate the tense gender relations of the samba universe. Lara rejected the notion that women could not occupy certain positions. Her most acclaimed album, *Sorriso Negro*, offers a ground for a critical discussion of the relation between samba, gender, and race in Brazil. Studying the pathbreaking career of this Afro-Brazilian woman who conquered the masculine world of samba composers is a way of understanding the complexity of contemporary Brazilian social relations.

Samba is a component and symbol of an extremely unequal society. As such, it follows trends and perceptions while, at the same time, creating and recreating its own rules of sociability. When Lara came of age, many Brazilian women were getting married early and focusing on becoming housewives. She chose to pursue professions that would give her financial stability and independence: nursing, social work, and songwriting. At her house, she was the breadwinner, at *rodas de samba*, a leader. Looking at the cover of the album *Samba, minha verdade, samba, minha raiz*, one can see a picture of Lara, surrounded by men, happily playing her *cavaquinho*. She did not ask for permission or pardon.

Despite her tenacity, Lara has never embraced any political engagement. She preferred melody to lyrics, lyricism to power, and conciliation to questioning. However, despite rejecting labels, her existence had a prominence for women and blacks in Brazil that many activists will never be able to reach. Moving slowly, but assertively, she overcame the machismo of samba and, in 1965, became the first woman to compose a *samba-enredo* at a large samba school. She attributed this to the fact that Império Serrano liked innovation, but she never refrained from mentioning her talent and, more importantly, her agency.

Artistic production is linked to collective creation, but also to subjectivity. Art is always a shared action, since the artist as an individual negotiates and elaborates his unique identity within a culture, codes and social relations of which he is part and which the artist also transforms with his work. The condition of the artist as a creative subject can only be properly understood if we can evaluate the socio-cultural space (traditions, customs, standards, values) in which he moves, not as an automaton but as a reinventor of codes and languages.[1]

Sorriso Negro is a consequence of the political moment Brazil faced at the time of its release. It has molded debates about black and female identity in the country. The public figure of Dona Ivone Lara, an example of *resistance by existence*, reshaped intersubjective understanding, impacting Brazilian society as a whole.

Between the moment the editor of this series, Jason Stanyek, first approached me to write this book and its publication, a lot has changed concerning gender roles in the world and Brazil. Of course, we already envisioned talking about *Sorriso Negro* in the context of the strengthening of the feminist and Black Movement in Brazil after *Abertura*; however, at that point, it did not seem that Lara's legacy would be as political as it is now. The MeToo movement has caused a shift in the paradigm. The attempts to deny racism in Brazil have never been as out of place as they are today. The commotion following the 2018 murder of councilwoman Marielle Franco in Rio de Janeiro is an example of this shift. Women and blacks are demanding representation and equality in universities, sports, and the film industry; across several fields it has ceased to be a discussion and became a need. Despite that (or maybe, in reaction to that), in October 2018, Brazilians rushed to the pools to confirm that they wanted Jair Bolsonaro to run the country. An overwhelming majority relied on a young democratic system to choose as president the man who said that the main mistake of the two-decade dictatorship was that "it did not kill enough people." In more than two decades serving as a congressman, Bolsonaro made several racist, misogynistic, and homophobic comments.

One of the messages I received the day of Lara's death was a link to a video in which the Brazilian mandolin player Hamilton de Holanda and the Portuguese singer Carminho performed "Nasci para sonhar e cantar" (I Was Born to Dream and to Sing), the title of my first book and one of my favorite songs. Besides the beautiful melody, the lyrics are a testimony to what Lara has represented for me. In the song, she says she was born to dream and sing, but also that she "needs" to reveal what is inside her as if this sentiment were stronger than anything else. I didn't listen to Holanda and Carminho's version immediately. Almost a week later, while reading the draft of the book, I clicked the link. All I could think of was Pretinho da Serrinha telling me that if one listens to Lara's songs with an open heart and closed eyes, it is impossible to hold back the tears. I cried. It was the melody, the lyrics, the perfectly imprecise mandolin, and Carminho's powerful voice making it feel like a Portuguese *fado*. But it was also a deep feeling of gratitude. After meeting Dona Ivone Lara, I learned to sew, received three master's degrees, finished a PhD, moved to New York, had a son, remarried, found love, drove an R.V., quit my job, played in a band, visited several countries—I challenged myself. Some of these things, I did pretty well. Others were disasters. But I did it all because I wanted to. I am sure I share my indebtedness to her with many Brazilians, even if unconsciously. Lara will always be remembered as the creator of melodies which embody the power of music. Her melodies help us understand love, death, hate, who we are, and who we do not want to be. They can convince us that the world is ours, if we want it to be.

Notes

Introduction

1 Law number 6.683 of August 28, 1979. Full text available online at http://www.planalto.gov.br/ccivil_03/leis/l6683.htm.

2 "A general loosens the reins in Brazil," *New York Times*, December 6, 1981.

3 Denise Rollemberg, *Exílio: Entre raízes e radares* (Rio de Janeiro: Record, 1999), 119–37; Teresa Cristina Schneider Marques, "Lembranças do exílio: as produções memorialísticas dos exilados pela ditadura militar brasileira," in *A construção da memória política*, Elias Medeiros and Naiara Molin (orgs.) (Pelotas-RS: UFPEL, 2011); Albertina de Oliveira Costa, Maria Teresa Porciúncula de Moraes, Norma Marzola, and Valentina da Rocha Lima (eds.), *Memórias das Mulheres do Exílio, Vol. 2* (Rio de Janeiro: Paz e Terra, 1980); and Pedro Uchôa Cavalcanti, Pedro Celso, and Jovelino Ramos (eds.), *Memórias do Exílio, 1964/19??: De muitos caminhos, Vol. 1* (São Paulo: Livramento, 1978).

4 Amelinha Teles and Rosalina Santa Cruz Leite, *Da guerrilha à imprensa feminista: a construção do feminismo pós-luta armada no Brasil (1975–1980)* (São Paulo: Editora Intermeios, 2013).

5 Medea Benjamin and Maisa Mendonça, *Benedita da Silva: An Afro-Brazilian Woman's Story of Politics and Love* (Oakland: Food First Books, 1997); and Michael Hanchard (ed.), *Racial Politics in Contemporary Brazil* (Durham: Duke University Press, 1999).

6 Paulina L. Alberto, *Terms of Inclusion: Black Intellectuals in Twentieth-Century Brazil* (Chapel Hill: The University of North Carolina Press, 2011).

7 Petrônio Domingues, "Movimento Negro Brasileiro: alguns apontamentos históricos," *Tempo* 12, no. 23 (2007): 100–22.

8 Ilma Fátima de Jesus, "O pensamento do MNU–Movimento Negro Unificado," in *O pensamento negro em educação no Brasil: expressões do movimento negro* (São Carlos: UFSCar, 1997).

9 Michael George Hanchard, *Orpheus and Power, The Movimento Negro of Rio de Janeiro and São Paulo, Brazil 1945–1988* (Princeton: Princeton University Press, 1994).

10 Interview with the author in Portuguese and translated by the author.

11 The works of Abdias do Nascimento that were actively informing the debate on race in Brazil at the time were, *O Genocídio do Negro Brasileiro* (Rio de Janeiro: Paz e Terra, 1978); *"Racial Democracy" in Brazil: Myth or Reality* (Ibadan: Sketch Publishers, 1977); *O Negro Revoltado* (Rio de Janeiro: Nova Fronteira, 1982), originally published in 1969; Abdias do Nascimento, Paulo Freire, and Nelson Werneck Sodré (orgs.), *Memórias do Exílio* (Lisboa: Arcádia, 1976). Edison Carneiro started his research on African-Brazilian culture earlier. See: Edison Carneiro, *Candomblés da Bahia* (Salvador: Editora do Museu do Estado da Bahia, 1948) and *Antologia do Negro Brasileiro* (Porto Alegre: Editora Globo, 1950).

12 Gilberto Freyre, *Casa-Grande e Senzala*, 50a edição revista (São Paulo: Global, 2005); *Sobrados e Mucambos*. 14a edição revista (São Paulo: Global, 2003); Caio Prado Junior,

Formação do Brasil contemporâneo (São Paulo: Brasiliense, 1996); Florestan Fernandes, *A integração do negro na sociedade de classes* (São Paulo: Editora Dominus/USP, 1964). More recently, controversy regarding the role of race in the construction of samba as a national symbol has illuminated the work of Marc Hertzman and Hermano Vianna. See Marc A. Hertzman, *Making Samba: A New History of Race and Music in Brazil* (Durham: Duke University Press, 2013); and Hermano Vianna, *O Mistério do Samba* (Rio de Janeiro: Jorge Zahar Editor and Editora UFRJ, 1995).

13 According to the *Oxford Dictionary*, activism is "the policy or action of using vigorous campaigning to bring about political or social change." Available online at: https://en.oxforddictionaries.com/definition/activism.

14 The discussion of activism in the arts is a fruitful one, which continues to inspire scholars. For more on this debate, see Chris Bobel, "'I'm not an activist, though I've done a lot of it': Doing activism, being activist and the 'perfect standard' in a contemporary movement," *Social Movement Studies* 6, no. 2 (2007): 147–59; and Karen Frostig, "Arts activism: Praxis in social justice, critical discourse, and radical modes of engagement," *Art Therapy* 28, no. 2 (2011): 50–56.

15 Stephen Bocskay, "Undesired presences: Samba, improvisation, and Afro-politics in 1970s Brazil," *Latin American Research Review* 52, no. 31 (2017): 64–78.

16 Candeia, "Sou mais Samba," in *Quatro Grandes do Samba* (Rio de Janeiro: RCA/BMG, 2001), 1 CD, Track 7.

17 Bocskay, "Undesired presences," 64–78.

18 For more about Rosinha de Valença, see http://dicionariompb.com.br/rosinha-de-valenca/dados-artisticos.

19 Juliana Ribeiro refers to the current debate about locus of enunciation or *lugar de fala* in Brazil. For more on that, see Djamila Ribeiro, *O que é lugar de fala* (Belo Horizonte: Letramento, 2017); and Ruth Wodak, *Discursive Construction of National Identity* (Edinburgh University Press, 2009), 75–83, in which the author investigates the anti-racist discourses in Brazil including ingroup and outgroup politics.

20 Interview with the author in Portuguese and translated by the author. For more on Clementina de Jesus, see Raquel Munhoz, *Quelé, a voz da cor: Biografia de Clementina de Jesus* (Rio de Janeiro: Civilização Brasileira, 2017).

21 Interview with the author in Portuguese and translated by the author.

22 Foucault states that "there is a plurality of resistances, each of them a special case: resistances that are possible, necessary, improbable; others that are spontaneous, savage, solitary, concerted, rampant, or violent; still others that are quick to compromise, interested, or sacrificial; by definition, they can only exist in the strategic field of power relations. But this does not mean that they are only a reaction or rebound, forming with respect to the basic domination an underside that is in the end always passive, doomed to perpetual defeat." See Michel Foucault, *The History of Sexuality, Volume 1: An Introduction* (New York: Pantheon Books, 1978), 96.

23 James C. Scott, *Domination and the Arts of Resistance: Hidden Transcripts* (New Haven: Yale University Press, 2010).

24 For more on the changes and applications of Foucault's concept of resistance, see Brent L. Pickett, "Foucault and the politics of resistance," *Polity* XXVIII, no. 4 (1996): 445–66;

and Irene Diamond, *Feminism and Foucault: Reflections on Resistance* (Lebanon, NH: Northeastern, 1988).

25 Mila Burns, *Nasci para sonhar e cantar: Dona Ivone Lara—a mulher no samba* (Rio de Janeiro: Record, 2009).

26 Ibid., 96.

27 Interview with the author in Portuguese and translated by the author.

28 I am using Henri Bergson's concept of *attention a la vie*. For more, see Henri Bergson, *Matter and Memory* (New York: Zone Books, 1988), 14; and David Lapoujade, "The normal and the pathological in Bergson," *MLN* 120, no. 5, Comparative Literature Issue (2005): 1146–55.

29 Hermínio Bello de Carvalho helped launch, in the 1960s, the career of Clementina de Jesus with the musical *Rosa de Ouro* as a producer and musical director. Born in 1935, he is also a writer, poet, and an expert in Brazilian music.

30 Interview with the author in Portuguese and translated by the author. Jovelina Pérola Negra (1944–1998) also was a housekeeper before becoming a singer and composer. Also from Império Serrano samba school, she is considered a prominent force in the *pagode* movement.

31 Interview with the author in Portuguese and translated by the author. For more on the multiple roles of women in the samba universe, see Rodrigo Cantos Savello Gomes, "Tias Baianas que lavam, cozinham, dançam, cantam, tocam e compõem: um exame das relações de gênero no samba da Pequena África do Rio de Janeiro na primeira metade do século XX," (presentation, I Simpósio Brasileiro de Pós-Graduandos em Música XV Colóquio do Programa de Pós-Graduação em Música da UNIRIO, Rio de Janeiro, 2010).

32 The *malandro* is a celebrated figure in the samba environment. In a loose translation, it would be the equivalent of the United States' hustler, trickster, or rascal character. But it is almost a symbol of Brazilian identity. For a broader debate on the topic, see Roberto da Matta, Carnavais, malandros e heróis: para uma sociologia do dilema brasileiro *(Rio de Janeiro: Rocco, 1979)*.

33 The *roda* is a "circle," the formation in which singers, instrumentalists, and the audience come together to perform samba. Several other African-Brazilian dance and musical forms also have a similar format, such as capoeira, *umbigada*, *maculelê*, and, as the name states, *samba de roda*.

34 Katia Santos, *Ivone Lara: a dona da melodia* (Rio de Janeiro: Editora Garamond, 2010), 89.

35 Maria Clementina Pereira Cunha, *Ecos da folia: Uma história social do carnaval carioca entre 1880 e 1920* (São Paulo: Editora Companhia das Letras, 2001); and Jota Efegê, *Figuras e coisas do Carnaval Carioca* (Rio de Janeiro: Funarte, 1982).

36 Burns, *Nasci para sonhar e cantar*, 43–51.

37 Ibid.

38 Ibid.

39 The I Congresso Nacional do Samba (First National Samba Congress), in 1962, defined that samba is "characterized by the use of the syncopation. Therefore, preserving the traditional characteristics of samba means appreciating the syncopation." In the 1970s, when *sambas-enredo* started to be compiled in albums every year, the songs became available to larger audiences, in addition to those who were in rehearsals and parties in the samba schools. Instead of small events where the samba community danced to support its school, the carnival parades had more and more participants. In such events, the school has a limited time to parade in an area ("cross the avenue," as Brazilians call it). If they exceed it, they lose points. Despite having more people to "cross," the schools were given the same time to do so as smaller groups. The solution was to speed up the tempo of samba to make sure everyone could pass on time. For more, see Carlos Sandroni, *Feitiço decente: transformações do samba no Rio de Janeiro (1917–1933)* (Rio de Janeiro: Jorge Zahar; Ed. UFRJ, 2001).

40 Interview with the author in Portuguese and translated by the author.

41 Translated by the author. In the original: "inclusive a de cultivadora de excelente linha melódica: D Ivone possui uma das mais sedutoras e quentes vozes negras da música popular brasileira." J. R. Tinhorão, "D Ivone Lara mostra em 'Sorriso Negro' suas qualidades de cantora," *Jornal do Brasil, Caderno B*, May 16th, 1981.

42 "Dona Ivone Lara supera equívocos," *Jornal do Brasil, Caderno B*, May 5th, 1981, 9.

43 Translated by the author. In the original, "insistem em apoiar o estilo tradicional da estrela com batidas e balanços ainda da bossa nova. Todos são ótimos, mas em cojunto dá pororoca." Ibid.

44 Fundo de Quintal was founded in 1980 by members of the Cacique de Ramos, a traditional and beloved carnival group in the suburb of Rio de Janeiro. It was initially formed by Almir Guineto, Jorge Aragão, Neoci, Sereno do Cacique, Sombrinha, Bira Presidente, Ubirany, Arlindo Cruz, and Valter Sete Cordas. Most of them would later become some of the most renowned Brazilian sambistas.

45 Cultural critic Tárik de Souza wrote, at the time of the release of Lara's fourth album *Alegria Minha Gente* (WEA), that *Sorriso Negro* only sold 5,000 copies. "Uma Cantora ainda Oculta pela Autora de Sucesso," *Jornal do Brasil, Caderno B*, August 30th, 1982, 2.

46 Interview with the author in Portuguese and translated by the author.

47 Ibid.

48 Ibid.

49 Bernardo Carneiro Horta, *Nise: Arqueóloga dos Mares* (E+A Edições do Autor, 2008).

50 Vianna, *O Mistério do Samba*, 129–36.

51 Interview with the author in Portuguese and translated by the author.

52 Ibid.

53 Leandro Braga, *Primeira Dama: A música de Dona Ivone Lara* (Rio de Janeiro: Gryphus, 2003).

54 Journalist Lucas Nobile states that she actually was 97 years old at the time of her death. He claims that her documents were altered by her family to be able to register her in school. See Lucas Nobile, *Dona Ivone Lara. A Primeira-Dama do Samba* (Rio de Janeiro: Sonora Editora, 2015).

Part 1

1 Interview with the author in Portuguese and translated by the author. In the original: "mulher não faz samba porque não vai a botequim."

2 *Mônica Velloso*, "As tias baianas tomam conta do pedaço . . . Espaço e identidade cultural no Rio de Janeiro," Estudos

Históricos *3, no. 6 (1990): 207–28;* Rodrigo Cantos Savello Gomes, "Samba no feminino: transformações das relações de gênero no samba carioca nas três primeiras décadas do Século XX" (master's thesis, Universidade do Estado de Santa Catarina, Florianopolis, 2011). Available online at http://tede.udesc.br/handle/handle/1590.

3   Roberto Moura, *Tia Ciata e a Pequena África no Rio de Janeiro* (Rio de Janeiro: Funarte, 1983), 93. Muniz Sodré compares the Praça Onze to the Congo Square, in New Orleans, an area where different people, references, and intersections meet, creating the place's uniqueness. See Muniz Sodré, *Samba, O dono do corpo* (Rio de Janeiro: Mauad, 1998), 17.

4   João do Rio, *As religiões no Rio* (1904), 15. Available online at http://www.dominiopublico.gov.br/download/texto/bi000185.pdf.

5   Ibid.

6   Lira Neto, *Uma história do samba: volume 1 (As Origens)* (São Paulo: Companhia das Letras, 2017), 41.

7   The samba school parade comprises of a series of segments known as *alas*. Each *ala* has several participants and tells part of the topic narrated in the samba-enredo. The *ala das baianas* is the only one that is mandatory. No matter the theme of the parade, it has to be present.

8   Dona Ivone Lara supera equívocos, "Bela para desfile, atrapalha Dona Ivone no seu jongar," *Jornal do Brasil, Caderno B*, May 5th, 1981, 9.

9   For more on this musical scene, see Jason Stanyek and Fabio Oliveira, "Nuances of Continual Variation in the Brazilian Pagode Song 'Sorriso Aberto,'" in *Analytical and Cross-Cultural Studies in World Music*, Michael Tenzer and John Roeder (eds.) (New York: Oxford University Press, 2011),

98–146; and Nilton Rodrigues Junior, "Pastoras na Voz, Insubmissas na Vida? As Mulheres da Velha Guarda da Portela," *Temiminós Revista Científica* 5, no. 1 (2015): 52–64.

10 At the heart of the power the *tias* exerted is slavery. The incorporation of black women to white families promoted a fragmentation of the black family. Mônica Pimenta Velloso explains that "the interests of the masters predominated, and they were more concerned with ensuring the reproduction of their labor-force. At the time of slavery, legislation always emphasized the "mother-child" unity, being more concerned with the separation of the children from the mother than from the father or from the separation between the spouses themselves. In this context, the mother ends up being responsible for the offspring, since the partners are always in transit." See Velloso, "As tias baianas tomam conta do pedaço," 207–28.

11 Ibid., 11.

12 Yls Rabelo Câmara, "Sereia Amazônica, Iara e Yemanjá, entidades aquáticas femininas dentro do folclore das Águas no Brasil," *Agália: Publicaçom internacional da Associaçom Galega da Lingua* 97/98 (2009): 115–30.

13 Aloysio de Oliveira (also known as Aloísio de Oliveira) was a singer, producer, composer, and a member of the group Bando da Lua, who played with Carmen Miranda in her international concerts. He is credited with the internationalization of Brazilian popular music. For more, see Aloysio de Oliveira, *De Banda pra lua* (Rio de Janeiro: Editora Record, 1982).

14 Translated by the author. In the original, "Eu era uma mulher que precisava de sorte, porque era a única contra um número enorme de violonistas, um bando de homens que não estava a fim de me ceder um lugar. Precisava quase arrancar as cordas do violão para que as pessoas compreendessem que eu sabia tocar. Quantas vezes fazia acordes fortíssimos para acordar as pessoas, para que calassem um pouco a boca e prestassem atenção: quando um artista toca ele tem que ser ouvido. Não importa que esteja de saia ou de cuecas." See Teresa Barros, "A Corda Forte de Rosinha de Valença," *Jornal do Brasil, Caderno B*, January 11, 1972, 4.

15 Interview with the author.

16 For a thorough investigation of the *samba de roda* of the Recôncavo Baiano, see Carlos Sandroni, *Samba de Roda do Recôncavo Baiano* (Instituto do Patrimônio Histórico e Artístico Nacional (IPHAN)). Available online at http://portal.iphan.gov.br/uploads/publicacao/ PatImDos_SambaRodaReconcavoBaiano_m.pdf. The report defines *samba de roda* as a musical and choreographic manifestation present in the entire state of Bahia, but particularly in the Recôncavo region. The participants are arranged in a rough circle format, performing a characteristic musical repertoire.

17 For a brief summary of the forms of samba, see Juvino Alves dos Santos Filho, "Ensaio sobre o samba," *Repertório* 43–46. Available online at http://www. revistarepertorioteatroedanca.tea.ufba.br/11/arq_pdf/ ensaiosobreosamba.pdf.

18 Flute and saxophone were the main instruments played by Alfredo da Rocha Viana, Jr., better known as Pixinguinha. One of the greatest Brazilian composers of all times, he helped popularize *choro* as a uniquely Brazilian genre.

For more, see André Diniz, *Pixinguinha: O Gênio e o Tempo* (São Paulo: Casa da Palavra, 2012).

19   Barbara Browning, *Samba: Resistance in Motion* (Bloomington: Indiana University Press, 1995), 9–10.

20   Sodré, *Samba, O dono do corpo*, 25.

21   Ibid.

22   José Ramos Tinhorão, *História Social da Música Popular Brasileira* (Rio de Janeiro: Editora 34, 1998), 99; and José Ramos Tinhorão, *Pequena História da Música Popular. Segundo Seus Gêneros* (Rio de Janeiro: Editora 34, 2013).

23   Interview with the author in Portuguese and translated by the author.

24   Those who practice the religion of Candomblé are usually designated "sons" and "daughters" of certain Orixás. Sons of Xangô are, in general, physically robust, full of energy and self-esteem. They are vigorous lovers, who are never satisfied with one partner. For more on Candomblé, see Carneiro, *Candomblés da Bahia*.

25   Xangô and Yansã are two of the Orixás, deities who represent a certain aspect of nature, the highest power in this Afro-Brazilian religion. Xangô is the god of fire, thunder, and justice. He wears rich ceremonial clothes and jewelry. His vibrant and fast dance refers to his regality and warrior nature. His colors are red and white. Yansã is the goddess of winds and storms. She is sensual, flirtatious, powerful, and authoritarian. Her dancing style refers to the movement of the wind and to battling. Her color is red. They both share a sacred day, Wednesday.

26   Interview with the author in Portuguese and translated by the author.

27   Interview with the author. The word *agogô* comes from Yoruba, meaning bell.

28   Note that in the original, Lara uses the word *saudade*, considered to have no direct translation to other languages. It means a feeling of nostalgia, longing, that many Brazilians and Portuguese attribute to their temperament.

29   Interview with the author in Portuguese and translated by the author.

30   Ibid.

31   In 1979, Elizeth Cardoso recorded "Unhas," the fourth track of *Sorriso Negro*, into the album *O inverno do meu tempo*. Cardoso mentored singer Francineth Germano, who in 1965 sang Lara's first recorded song, "Amor Inesquecível" (Unforgetable Love).

32   Carmen Costa (1920–2007) was a singer and composer born in the state of Rio de Janeiro. She became widely known in the Brazilian Radio Era and her first hit was a version of the Mexican song Cielito Lindo titled "Está Chegando a Hora" (The Time is Coming). In the mid-1940s she married an American citizen, Hans Van Koehler, and moved to the United States. In 1962, she sang at the famous bossa nova concert at Carnegie Hall, in New York, with Tom Jobim, João Gilberto, Stan Getz, and others.

33   Translated by the author. In the original: "uma das mais bem sucedidas herdeiras de um estilo de interpretação negro-brasileira que tem num extremo o diamante bruto da voz de Clementina de Jesus, e, no outro, o brilho de ônix dos puros concentrados graves da voz de Carmen Costa," *Jornal do Brasil, Caderno B*, May 16th, 1981.

34 Interview with the author in Portuguese and translated by the author.

35 Ibid.

36 Luís da Câmara Cascudo, *Dicionário do Folclore Brasileiro* (Rio de Janeiro: Ed. Ediouro, 1954). Translated by the author.

37 For more information about *ranchos*, see Cunha, *Ecos da folia*; and Efegê, *Figuras e coisas do Carnaval Carioca*.

38 Burns, *Nasci para sonhar e cantar*, 48.

39 Ibid.

40 Interview with the author in Portuguese and translated by the author.

41 "Zaíra de Oliveira," Dicionário Cravo Albin da Música Popular Brasileira. Available online at http://dicionariompb.com.br/zaira-de-oliveira/.

42 Ibid.

43 Interview with the author in Portuguese and translated by the author.

44 Ibid.

45 Ibid.

46 Marília T. Barboza da Silva and Arthur L. de Oliveira Filho, *Silas de Oliveira, do jongo ao samba-enredo* (Rio de Janeiro: Funarte, 1981), 29. *Calango* is a musical rhythm originally from rural areas in Rio, to which couples dance at balls; *blocos* are street bands followed by a crowd, a very popular part of carnival festivities; the *pastorinhas* are a group of women who sing, normally church songs, in the streets of the city; *jongo* is a dance originally from Africa and still preserved in the area of Serrinha, in which percussive instruments are central, as well as manifestations of

Afro-Brazilian culture; *pagode* is a subgenre of samba, also originally from Rio de Janeiro.

47 The effects of the Great Depression and the long-lasting crisis of the Old Republic were strongly felt in 1930s Brazil, and the political climate led rebels to question the election of the São Paulo establishment candidate, Júlio Prestes. Getúlio Vargas, supported by industrialists, the reformist sector of the military, and landowners from other states, gained support for a military *coup*. For more on this, see Boris Fausto, *A Revolução de 1930, Historiografia e História* (São Paulo: Companhia das Letras, 1997).

48 Sérgio Cabral, "Getúlio Vargas e a música popular brasileira," *Ensaios de opinião*, Rio de Janeiro 3, nos. 2/1 (1975): 36–41.

49 Interview with the author in Portuguese and translated by the author.

50 Horta, *Nise*.

51 That same year, members of Prazer da Serrinha discontent with Alfredo Costa's authoritarianism and his decision over a samba-enredo decided to create Império Serrano, which became a force in Rio de Janeiro's carnival.

52 Interview with the author in Portuguese and translated by the author.

53 Burns, *Nasci para sonhar e cantar*, 85.

54 Interview with the author. Tia Tira, Iraci Cardoso dos Santos, was considered to be the "pilar da Serrinha," or the "cornerstone" of the Serrinha community. She was a midwife, a healer, and carried the traditions of *jongo* in the community.

55 Marilda Santanna (ed.), *As bambas do samba: mulher e poder na roda* (Salvador: Edfba, 2016). Translated by the author.

56 Ibid.

57 Interview with the author in Portuguese and translated by the author.

58 Interview with the author.

59 Translation by the author.

60 Nei Lopes, "Afro-Brazilian Music and Identity." *Conexoes: African Diaspora Research Project* 5, no. 1 (1993): 6–8.

61 Interview with the author in Portuguese and translated by the author.

62 The festival took place in the same year when the Institutional Act Number Five was enforced and censorship became the rule in Brazil. The song "Sabiá," by Tom Jobim and Chico Buarque, won the competition despite the complaints of the audience. The song talked about exile in metaphors and did not catch the audience. "Para Não Dizer que Não Falei de Flores," by Geraldo Vandré, became the anthem of resistance to the military regime, and was the favorite one, but placed second in the festival.

63 Philip Galinsky, "Co-option, cultural resistance, and Afro–Brazilian identity: A history of the 'pagode' samba movement in Rio de Janeiro," *Latin American Music Review/ Revista de Música Latinoamericana* 17, no. 2 (Autumn–Winter, 1996): 120.

64 Céli Regina Jardim Pinto, *Uma história do feminismo no Brasil* (São Paulo: Editora Fundação Perseu Abramo, 2003), 13–14.

65 Ibid., 21–28.

66 Burns, *Nasci para sonhar e cantar*, 96.

67 Bergson, *Matter and Memory*, 14. For more on the discussion of Bergson's *attention a la vie*, see Lapoujade, "The normal and the pathological in Bergson," 1146–55.

68   Alfred Schütz, *The Phenomenology of the Social World* *(Evanston: Northwestern University Press, 1967).*

69   Heleieth Saffioti, *A Mulher na Sociedade de Classes Mito e Realidade* (Petrópolis: Vozes, 1976).

70   Isabel Cristina Hentz and Ana Maria Veiga, "Entre o feminismo e a esquerda: contradições e embates da dupla militância," in *Resistências, Gênero e Feminismos contra as ditaduras no Cone Sul*, Joana Maria Pedro, Cristina Scheibe Wolff, and Ana Maria Veiga (orgs.) (Florianópolis: Editora Mulheres, 2011), 145–164

71   Writer Mario Magalhães recalls several of the protest signs, including, "The old men in power, the young ones in the coffin," in the article "Mataram um estudante, ele podia ser seu filho. Há 50 anos, um assassinato comoveu o Brasil. E se fosse hoje?" *The Intercept*, February, 28, 2018. Available online at: https://theintercept. com/2018/02/28/mataram-um-estudante-ele-podia-ser-seu-filho-ha-50-anos-um-assassinato-comoveu-o-brasil-e-se-fosse-hoje/.

72   Maria Amélia de Almeida Teles, *Breve História do Feminismo no Brasil* (São Paulo: Editora Brasiliense, 1993).

73   "A Revolta das Mães," *Correio da Manhã*, September 12, 1968. Available online at http://memoria.bn.br/DocReader/ Hotpage/HotpageBN.aspx?bib=089842_07&pagfis=95478& url=http://memoria.bn.br/docreader#.

74   Ibid.

75   Torture, murder, and imprisonment were part of a policy intensified after the Institutional Act Number Five (Ato Institucional Número Cinco, AI-5). The decree gave President Artur da Costa e Silva the authority to order the National Congress and the State Legislative Assemblies into forced recess. Under the pretext of "national security," it authorized the government to appoint federal officers (*interventores*) to run states and municipalities. They censored the press, music, movies, theater, and television. The AI-5 also determined political meetings to be illegal and suspended habeas corpus for crimes of political motivation. Official data attest that this was the most violent period of the Brazilian dictatorship, with more than 400 deaths. For more information, see Centro de Pesquisa e Documentação (CPDOC) Fundação Getulio Vargas, Document ACM pm 1964.04.09, 09/04/1964 – 04/1975 microfilm 1 fot. 619 to 629; and *Direito à verdade e à memória: Comissão Especial sobre Mortos e Desaparecidos Políticos* (Brasília: Secretaria Especial dos Direitos Humanos, 2007), 89. Available online at http://www.dhnet.org.br/dados/livros/a_pdf/livro_memoria1_direito_verdade.pdf.

76 Teles, *Breve História do Feminismo no Brasil*.

77 Ibid., 71–73. The *Guerrilha do Araguaia* (Araguaia Guerrilla) was an armed group who fought against the dictatorship between 1967 and 1974 in North and Northeast Brazil. Founded by militants of the Communist Party of Brazil (PC do B) it planned to create a rural revolution against the military regime.

78 Ibid.

79 Teles and Leite, *Da guerrilha à imprensa feminists*, 59–67.

80 Ibid., 65.

81 Pinto, *Uma história do feminismo no Brasil*, 73.

82 Angela Neves-Xavier de Brito, "Brazilian women in exile: The quest for an identity," *Latin American Perspectives* 13, no. 2 (1986): 58–80.

83 Ibid., 67.

84 Gislene Aparecida dos Santos, *Mulher negra, homem branco.*
Um breve estudo do feminino negro (Rio de Janeiro: Pallas,
2004), 39.

85 Yvonne Maggie, *Guerra de Orixá. Um estudo de ritual e*
conflito (Rio de Janeiro: Jorge Zahar Editor, 2001).

86 Interview with the author.

87 Ibid.

Part 2

1 Interview with the author.

2 Paulinho da Viola, *Nervos de Aço* (Rio de Janeiro: Odeon,
1973).

3 For an inquiry of two covers of Paulinho da Viola's albums
released during the dictatorship, see Paula Paraíso
Porciúncula, *A Dança da Solidão* (1972) *e Nervos de Aço*
(1973)*: a arte nas capas de discos durante a ditadura no*
Brasil (TCC, Universidade Federal de Santa Catarina, 2016).
Available online at https://repositorio.ufsc.br/xmlui/
bitstream/handle/123456789/179608/TCC_Paula_Paraiso_
Porciuncula_2016_1.pdf?sequence=1&isAllowed=y.

4 Chico Buarque de Hollanda, *Construção* (Rio de Janeiro:
Marola Edições Musicais, 1971).

5 Interview with the author in Portuguese and translated by
the author.

6 Ibid.

7 Ibid.

8 Ibid.

9 Ibid.

10 Tinhorão, *História Social da Música Popular Brasileira*, 311.

11 Thais Lobo, "'Bossa nova é ritmo de goteira,' diz Tinhorão na Flip," *O Globo*, May 7, 2015. Available online at https://oglobo.globo.com/cultura/livros/bossa-nova-ritmo-de-goteira-diz-tinhorao-na-flip-16668223#ixzz5BFdEoRrF.

12 Ibid.

13 Television, and more specifically TV Record, dedicated a large portion of the programming to Brazilian music. Two of its most successful shows are examples of the trend at the time: *Fino da Bossa*, focusing on bossa nova, and *Jovem Guarda*, dedicated to Brazilian rock and roll. See Valéria Guimarães, "A passeata contra a guitarra e a 'autêntica' música brasileira," in *Identidades brasileiras: composições e recomposições,* Cristina Carneiro Rodrigues, Tania Regina de Luca, and Valéria Guimarães (orgs.) (São Paulo: Editora UNESP, 2014), 145–73.

14 *Uma noite em 67*, directed by Ricardo Calil and Renato Terra (Rio de Janeiro: VideoFilmes, 2010), DVD. For more on the Chilean Nueva Canción's perspective, see Patrick Barr-Melej, *Psychedelic Chile: Youth, Counterculture, and Politics on the Road to Socialism and Dictatorship* (Chapel Hill: The University of North Carolina Press, 2017).

15 Ibid.

16 Andrade states that "Brazilian music is the most complete, the most totally national, strongest creation of our race until now." See Mário de Andrade, *Ensaio sobre a música brasileira* (São Paulo: Vila Rica; Brasília: INL, 1972). Available online at http://www.ufrgs.br/cdrom/mandrade/mandrade.pdf.

17 Eduardo Vicente, "Segmentação e consumo: a produção fonográfica brasileira – 1965–1999," *ArtCultura* 10, no. 16 (2008): 103–12. Available online at http://producao.usp.br/handle/BDPI/32361.

18 Ibid. Translated by the author.

19 Ibid., 111.

20 Ibid., 107.

21 Santos, *Ivone Lara: a dona da melodia*, 75.

22 Amaury Monteiro, *O Globo*, December 2, 1972. Cited in Silva and de Oliveira Filho, *Silas de Oliveira, do jongo ao samba-enredo*, 111.

23 Burns, *Nasci para sonhar e cantar*, 112.

24 Ibid.

25 Interview with the Museu da Imagem e do Som, Rio de Janeiro, 23 de julho de 2008, "Projeto depoimentos para posteridade do MIS."

26 For more on bossa nova and Tropicália, see Santuza Cambraia Naves, *Da bossa nova à tropicália* (Rio de Janeiro: Zahar, 2001).

27 "Silas de Oliveira, autor de 'Aquarela brasileira,' um dos bambas do samba," *O Globo*, September 30, 2016. Available online at http://acervo.oglobo.globo.com/em-destaque/silas-de-oliveira-autor-de-aquarela-brasileira-um-dos-bambas-do-samba-20208211#ixzz59MsdnfV3.

28 Silva and de Oliveira Filho, *Silas de Oliveira, do jongo ao samba-enredo*, 94.

29 Burns, *Nasci para sonhar e cantar*, 107.

30 Ibid.

Notes

31 Haroldo Costa, *Salgueiro: Academia do Samba* (Rio de Janeiro: Record, 1984).

32 Interview with the author in Portuguese and translated by the author.

33 Ibid.

34 Silva and de Oliveira Filho, *Silas de Oliveira, do jongo ao samba-enredo*, 34.

35 Ibid., 35.

36 The standard tuning of a cavaquinho in Brazil is D G B D, while the mandolin's is G D A E.

37 "Sambabook – Dona Ivone Lara," compilation, Universal Music, DVD, 2015.

38 Ibid.

39 Silva and de Oliveira Filho, *Silas de Oliveira, do jongo ao samba-enredo*, 115.

40 Ibid., 116.

41 Ibid., 111.

42 "Silas de Oliveira, autor de 'Aquarela brasileira,' um dos bambas do samba," *O Globo*, September 30, 2016. Available online at http://acervo.oglobo.globo.com/em-destaque/silas-de-oliveira-autor-de-aquarela-brasileira-um-dos-bambas-do-samba-20208211#ixzz5Ayb5A28O.

43 Burns, *Nasci para sonhar e cantar*, 113.

44 Ibid.

45 Ibid., 114.

46 Interview with the author in Portuguese and translated by the author.

47 Burns, *Nasci para sonhar e cantar*, 118–19.

48 Ibid., 119.

49 Interview with the author in Portuguese and translated by the author.

50 Ibid.

51 Nobile, *Dona Ivone Lara. A Primeira-Dama do Samba*, 100.

52 Ibid.

53 http://dicionariompb.com.br/clementina-de-jesus/biografia.

54 Translated by the author. In the original: "Ora, como se sabe, esganar é matar por sufocação. Ao que tudo indica, sufocar um coração com o bico, nem o carcará de João do Vale." The critic is referring to the protest song "Carcará," by João do Vale and José Cândido, which was the main song of the musical play *Opinião* (Opinion). It helped launch Maria Bethânia's career in 1965. The song was the first one Bethânia recorded and released as a professional singer and hers is still remembered as a pathbreaking interpretation. Tinhorão, "D Ivone Lara mostra em 'Sorriso Negro' suas qualidades de cantora."

55 Interview with the author in Portuguese and translated by the author.

56 Ibid.

57 The show was broadcast by TV Brasil. The part in which they talk about "Tendência" is available at https://www.youtube.com/watch?v=ilOZXwRB8C4.

58 Interview with the author in Portuguese and translated by the author.

59 João Pimentel, *Jorge Aragão: O Enredo de um Samba* (Rio de Janeiro: Sonora Edições, 2016).

60 Interview with the author in Portuguese and translated by the author.

61 When interviewing Bira Presidente, I expected he would fill the gaps in my research, letting me know who were the musicians playing in the album. However, he attested that he could not recall because he had recorded with Lara in almost all her works. I told him I had found some reviews of the concert *Sorriso Negro* that mentioned him playing, but none about the album. He then stated that he recalled the concert and assumed he and his peers of Fundo de Quintal were also in the recording.

62 The use of the freight elevator, called "service elevator" in Brazil, is not only related to the carrying of heavy weight or dirty materials. It is also supposed to be used by domestic workers and has been evidence and a symbol of racism in several instances, including some in which upper-class black people were directed to the freight elevator.

Part 3

1 The songs and hymns of the church were recorded on the album *Rosário Dos Pretos —Cânticos*, compilation, 1999.

2 A Third Order is an association of religious people who follow the ideals and spirit of the Catholic church, but do not belong to the First Order (for example, Dominicans, Franciscans, and Augustinian friars) nor to the Second Order (cloistered nuns).

3 The United Nations attests that "the city has managed to preserve many outstanding Renaissance buildings.

A special feature of the old town are the brightly colored houses, often decorated with fine stucco-work." See https://whc.unesco.org/en/list/309.

4 The church prides itself on celebrating Afro-Brazilian culture while being a Catholic church. The official website stated that it is "a non-profit religious association of Catholic people of both sexes, of black color, of unblemished conduct, and who practice as good Christians the commandments of God and the Church. Throughout the time this Brotherhood ended up acquiring a cultural aspect, since it has always been a space of strengthening and preservation of Afro-Brazilian culture and identity" (available at http://irmandaderosariodospretossalvador.blogspot.com/ in Portuguese and translated by the author). For more on the history of black lay brotherhoods devoted to Nossa Senhora do Rosário, see Luis Monteiro da Costa, "A devoção de Nossa Senhora do Rosário na Cidade do Salvador," *Revista do Instituto Genealógico da Bahia* 10, no. 10 (1958): 95–113.

5 For more on black lay brotherhoods in Bahia, see: Jefferson Bacelar and Maria Conceição B. de Souza, *O Rosário dos Pretos do Pelourinho* (Salvador: Fundação do Patrimônio Artístico e Cultural da Bahia, 1974); Roger Bastide, *As religiões africanas no Brasil* (São Paulo: Pioneira/USP, 1971); Manoel S. Cardozo, "The lay brotherhoods of colonial Bahia," *Catholic Historical Review* 33, no. 1 (1947): 12–30; and Patricia Mulvey, "The black lay brotherhoods of colonial Brazil: A history" (Ph.D. Dissertation, City University of New York, 1976).

6 Carlos Ott, "A Irmandade do Nossa Senhora do Rosário dos Pretos do Pelourinho," *Afro-Ásia* 6–7 (1968): 120.

7 João José Reis, "Identidade e diversidade étnicas nas irmandades negras no tempo da escravidão," *Tempo* 2, no. 3 (1996), 7–33: 18. Translated by the author.

8 Lucilene Reginaldo, *Os rosários dos angolas—irmandades de africanos e crioulos na Bahia setecentista* (São Paulo: Alameda, 2011).

9 Alexandre Vieira Ribeiro compares the different estimates provided by several historians in "Estimativas sobre o volume do tráfico Transatlântico de escravos para a Bahia, 1582–1851." Available online at http://anais.anpuh.org/wp-content/uploads/mp/pdf/ANPUH.S23.1078.pdf.

10 L. A. Costa Pinto, *Recôncavo—Laboratório de Uma Experiência Humana* (Rio de Janeiro: Centro Latino-Americano de Pesquisas em Ciências Sociais, Publicação número 1, 1958).

11 J. Velloso produced the album *Rosário Dos Pretos—Cânticos* in 1999 and "Sorriso Negro" is the 14th track. Other celebrated black artists, such as Chico César, Filhos de Gandhi, Dona Edith do Prato, Margareth Menezes, and Olodum also recorded songs in the album.

12 Interview with the author in Portuguese and translated by the author. For more on the discussion about locus of enunciation or *lugar de fala* in Brazil, see Ribeiro, *O que é lugar de fala*. On page 8, she asserts that "there is no determined epistemology specifically about the term *lugar de fala*; the origin of the term is imprecise, but we believe it comes from the traditions of discourses about 'feminist stand point,' diversity, racial critical theory, and decolonization theory." Also see Wodak, *Discursive Construction of National Identity*, 75–83.

13   Santos, Thereza. "The black movement: without identity there is no consciousness or struggle." *UCLA Latin American studies* 86 (1999): 23–30.

14   For more on the debate that sought to bring to light racism in Brazil and debunk the myth of racial democracy, see Abdias do Nascimento, *O negro revoltado* (Rio de Janeiro: Editora Nova Fronteira, 1982); Abdias do Nascimento, "O genocídio do negro brasileiro," in *O Brasil na mira do pan-africanismo*, Abdias do Nascimento (ed.) (Salvador: EDUFBA/CEAO, 2002); France Winddance Twine, *Racism in a Racial Democracy: The Maintenance of White Supremacy in Brazil* (New Brunswick: Rutgers University Press, 1998).

15   Patricia Hill Collins, *On Intellectual Activism* (Philadelphia: Temple University Press, 2013), ix.

16   Katia Regina da Costa Santos, "Dona Ivone Lara: Voz e Corpo da Síncopa do Samba" (Ph.D. Thesis, University of Georgia, 2005), 96. Available at https://getd.libs.uga.edu/pdfs/santos_katia_c_200505_phd.pdf.

17   Ibid.

18   Interview with the author in Portuguese and translated by the author.

19   Ibid.

20   The artist changed his name to Jorge Ben Jor in 1989. For more, see Pedro Alexandre Sanches, "Jorge Ben Jor, o Homen Patropi," *Revista Trip*, November 10, 2009, 15–26.

21   Ibid.

22   Luiz Tatit, *O Século da Canção* (Cotia: Ateliê Editorial, 2004), 229.

23 Christopher Dunn, *Brutality Garden: Tropicalia and the Emergence of a Brazilian Counterculture* (Chapel Hill: The University of North Carolina Press, 2014).

24 Alexandre Reis dos Santos, "Eu quero ver quando Zumbi chegar: negritude, política e relações raciais na obra de Jorge Ben (1963–1976)" (M.A. thesis, History Department, Universidade Federal Fluminense, 2014).

25 In an article about *África Brasil*, Luciana Xavier de Oliveira argues that "after *África Brasil*, the composer begins to depart from the compositional style that characterizes Brazilian Popular Music (MPB) to approach a pop sonority. From this moment on, he aims at a broader market, also seeking to reach discos and a younger audience, using bolder marketing strategies to reach higher sales rates and consolidate his place within the mainstream of Brazilian music" (translated by the author). See Luciana Xavier de Oliveira, "África Brasil (1976): uma análise midiática do album de Jorge Ben Jor," *Contemporanea-Revista de Comunicação e Cultura* 10, no. 1 (2012), 158–74: 164.

26 Chica da Silva (or Xica da Silva) was born in 1732 in Minas Gerais. She was the topic of movies, telenovelas, carnival parades, and of several scholarly works. See Júnia Ferreira Furtado, *Chica da Silva: A Brazilian Slave of the Eighteenth Century* (New York: Cambridge University Press, 2008).

27 Zumbi was also the central figure in one of the most famous sambas-enredo of Vila Isabel, "Kizomba, festa da raça" (1988), by Rodolpho, Jonas e Luís Carlos da Vila. See Marcelo de Mello, *O enredo do meu samba—a história de quinze sambas-enredo imortais* (Rio de Janeiro: Record, 2015).

28 Interview with the author in Portuguese and translated by the author.

29 More recently, however, scholars began to point to it as potentially a different form of activism, similar to what I call *resistance by existence*. The main source in this debate is Scott's, *Domination and the Arts of Resistance*. For a particular debate of the concept in Armstrong's career, see Melanie Reiff, "Unexpected activism: A study of Louis Armstrong and Charles Mingus as activists using James Scott's theory of public versus hidden transcripts," *Sound Ideas—Summer Research*, Paper 55, 2010.

30 Marília Gessa and Derek Pardue, *Racionais MCs' Sobrevivendo no Inferno* (New York: Bloomsbury Academic, Forthcoming).

31 Interview with the author in Portuguese and translated by the author.

32 Interview with the Museu da Imagem e do Som, Rio de Janeiro, July 23, 2008, "Projeto depoimentos para posteridade do MIS." Translated by the author.

33 Ibid.

34 Ibid.

35 Giorgia Cavicchioli, "Leci Brandão: Todas nós, mulheres negras, temos a mesma história," *IstoÉ*, March 30, 2018. Available online at https://istoe.com.br/leci-brandao-todas-nos-mulheres-negras-temos-a-mesma-historia/.

36 Interview with the author in Portuguese and translated by the author.

37 Ibid.

38 Ibid.

39 Antônio Candeia Filho, "Sou mais o samba–Candeia." Available online at https://www.youtube.com/watch?v=6DORm-WIO6Q (accessed April 7, 2018).

40   Bocskay, "Undesired presences," 74.

41   Thomas E. Skidmore, *The Politics of Military Rule in Brazil, 1964–1985* (New York: Oxford University Press, 1990), 73–84.

42   Paulina L. Alberto, "When Rio was Black: Soul music, national culture, and the politics of racial comparison in 1970s Brazil," *Hispanic American Historical Review* 89, no. 1 (2009): 3–39.

43   Lena Frias, "Black Rio: O orgulho (importado) de ser negro no Brasil," *Jornal do Brasil*, July 17, 1976.

44   For more on the debate, see Hanchard, *Orpheus and Power*; Twine, *Racism in a Racial Democracy*; and George Reid Andrews, *Blacks & Whites in São Paulo, Brazil, 1888–1988* (Madison: University of Wisconsin Press, 1991).

45   Alberto, "When Rio was Black." The Black Rio movement mobilized legions of Afro-Brazilians in the 1970s. Initially inspired by US funk music, the movement went beyond music to become a social and political revolution that aimed to affirm black pride and reject racism and racial inequality. Musicians such as Tim Maia, Cassiano, Hyldon, Gerson King Combo, Dom Mita, Sandra de Sá, and Toni Tornado, and groups like Banda Black Rio and Banda União Black, are some of the most prominent names of the movement. For more information, see Luiz Felipe de Lima Peixoto and Zé Octavio Sebadelhe, *1976: Movimento Black Rio* (Rio de Janeiro: José Olympio, 2016); and Christopher Dunn, *Contracultura* (Chapel Hill: The University of North Carolina Press, 2016).

46   Dmitri Cerboncini Fernandes, "A negra essencialização do samba," *Luso-Brazilian Review* 51–1 (2014): 132–56.

47   For more on the debate, see Santos, "The Black movement"; Nascimento, *O negro revoltado*; Thomas E. Skidmore,

Black into White: Race and Nationality in Brazilian Thought (Durham: Duke University Press, 1993); *Race, Class, and Power in Brazil*, ed. Pierre-Michel Fontaine (Los Angeles: Center for Afro-American Studies, UCLA, 1985); and Helene Monteiro, "O ressurgimento do movimento Negro no Rio de Janeiro na década de 70" (Master's thesis, Universidade Federal do Rio de Janeiro, 1991).

48 For more on the transitions experienced in the samba schools at this time and the current structure of the carnival parade in Rio de Janeiro, see Maria Laura Viveiros de Castro Cavalcanti, *Carnaval carioca: dos bastidores ao desfile* (Rio de Janeiro: Funarte; UFRJ, 1994).

49 The Inconfidência Mineira, Minas Gerais Conspiracy, was an unsuccessful separatist movement in 1789, when Brazil was a Portuguese colony. Its leader was Joaquim José da Silva Xavier, known as Tiradentes, considered today as one of the most important historical figures in the country.

50 Chico Otavio and Aloy Jupiara, "Sambas-enredo enfrentaram o regime militar," *O Globo*, September 10, 2013. The story also mentions the censorship of a song by Martinho da Vila and the monitoring of samba school Salgueiro.

51 Vianna, *O Mistério do Samba*, 129–36.

52 For more on the law, see Monica Grin and Marcos Chor Maio, "O antirracismo da ordem no pensamento de Afonso Arinos de Melo Franco," *Topoi* 14, no. 26 (2013): 33–45. The authors argue that "Arinos sought to shift the racial question from a political debate to a moral issue. The fight against racism, once translated into ethical mores inspired by the traditional view of a racially harmonic country, should inhibit the rising atmosphere of racial conflict rather than recognize the Black movement's sociopolitical demands."

53 Afonso Arinos, *Obra completa* (Rio de Janeiro: Conselho Federal de Cultura, 1969), 883–95.

54 In 1946, Leon L. Matthias wrote a review of Freyre's book *The American Catholic Sociological Review* in which he declared that the work "belongs to the immortal class of Humboldt's *New Spain*, Tocqueville's *Democracy*, Leroy-Beaulieu's *Russia*, Rivers' *Melanesia*, or Taine's *England*." See Leon L. Matthias, "Book review: Masters and slaves," *The American Catholic Sociological Review* 7, no. 4 (December, 1946): 282–84.

55 Freyre, *Casa-Grande e Senzala*, 78. The Jesuits founded missions throughout the interior Brazil, developing infrastructure that was the base for Brazilian cities. Portuguese King João III sent the Catholic order Society of Jesus to the then colony in 1549 in an attempt to colonize and develop it. Their mission was to educate and evangelize indigenous groups, and its system included the forced labor of native people and their conversion to Catholicism.

56 This idea was also central to the development of the Brazilian Modernist Movement. For more on music during this period, see Santuza Cambraia Naves, *O Violão Azul. Modernismo e Música Popular* (Rio de Janeiro: Fundação Getulio Vargas, 1998).

57 Emília Viotti da Costa, *Da senzala à colônia* (São Paulo: Unesp, 1998).

58 Sérgio Buarque de Holanda, *Roots of Brazil* (Notre Dame, IN: Notre Dame Press, 2012).

59   Florestan Fernandes, *Capitalismo Dependente e Classes Sociais na América Latina* (Rio de Janeiro: Zahar, 1973); and Florestan Fernandes, *A integração do negro na sociedade de classes* (São Paulo: Dominus, 1965).

60   One of the main critiques of Paul Gilroy's *The Black Atlantic* is that it excludes from the narrative Brazil, the country of the Atlantic with the largest enslaved population. It can be perceived as yet another endeavor to interpret the country as a mere receiver of external influence, a narrative that several scholars have questioned, criticized, and ultimately proved to be insufficient. Paul Gilroy, *The Black Atlantic: Modernity and Double Consciousness* (Cambridge, MA: Harvard University Press, 1993). For an attempt to decentralize the narrative from the Civil Rights Movement, see: Amílcar Araújo Pereira, "Influências externas, circulação de referenciais e a constituição do movimento negro contemporâneo no Brasil: idas e vindas no 'Atlântico Negro,'" *Ciências e Letras*, Porto Alegre, no. 44 (2008): 215–36; Patricia de Santana Pinho, "Descentrando os Estados Unidos nos estudos sobre negritude no Brasil," *Revista Brasileira de Ciências Sociais* 20, no. 59 (2005): 37–50; Livio Sansone, "Negritudes e racismos globais? Uma tentativa de relativizar alguns dos novos paradigmas 'universais' nos estudos da etnicidade a partir da realidade brasileira," *Horizontes Antropológicos* 4, no. 8 (1998): 227–37; Sabrina Gledhill, "Expandindo as margens do Atlântico Negro: Leituras sobre Booker T. Washington no Brasil," *Revista de História Comparada* 7, no. 2 (2013): 122–48.

61   Amílcar Araújo Pereira, "Linhas (da cor) cruzadas: relações raciais, imprensa negra e Movimento Negro no Brasil e nos Estados Unidos," in *O Movimento Negro Brasileiro: escritos* *sobre os sentidos de democracia e justiça social no Brasil*, Amauri Mendes Pereira and Joselina da Silva (orgs.) (Belo Horizonte: Nandyala, 2009), 109–26.

62 Important institutions of resistance were born during the regime, such as the Centro de Cultura e Arte Negra (CECAN), founded in 1972; the black newspapers *Árvore das Palavras* (1974), *O Quadro* (1974), and *Nagô* (1975); and the Instituto de Pesquisa das Culturas Negras (IPCN), created in 1976. For more, see Domingues, "Movimento Negro Brasileiro," 100–22.

63 Joel Rufino dos Santos. "O movimento negro e a crise brasileira." *Politica e administração* 2, no. 2 (1985): 287–307.

64 The organization Convergência Socialista published *Versus*, which included a section called "Afro-Latino America." For more information, see David Covin, "Afrocentricity in O Movimento Negro Unificado," *Journal of Black Studies* 21, no. 2 (1990): 126–44.

65 Lélia Gonzalez, "The unified Black movement: A new stage in Black political mobilization," in *Race, Class, and Power in Brazil*, Pierre-Michel Fontaine (ed.) (Los Angeles: UCLA, 1985).

66 Verena Alberti and Amílcar Araújo Pereira (eds.), *Histórias do movimento negro no Brasil: depoimentos ao CPDOC* (Rio de Janeiro: Pallas Editora, 2007).

67 Gonzalez, "The unified Black movement," 125.

68 de Jesus, "O pensamento do MNU–Movimento Negro Unificado."

69 de Lima Peixoto and Sebadelhe, *1976: Movimento Black Rio*; and Dunn, *Contracultura*.

70 *Pequeno Dicionário Houaiss da língua portuguesa* (São Paulo: Editora Moderna, 2015).

71 "Projeto Kalunga: a música brasileira em Angola," *O Globo*, May 14, 1980.

72 Stories, pictures, and interviews about Project Kalunga are online as part of the Memória do Projeto Kalunga, in the archives of the Museu Afro-Digital. Available at http://www.museuafrorio.uerj.br/?work=memoria-do-projeto-kalunga.

73 Dulcy Tupi, *Foi bonita a festa pá*. Available online at http://www.museuafrorio.uerj.br/?work=memoria-do-projeto-kalunga.

74 Ibid.

75 Ibid.

76 Rachel Teixeira Valença and Suetônio Soares Valença, *Serra, Serrinha, Serrano, o império do samba* (Rio de Janeiro: Livraria José Olympio Editora, 1981).

77 For a discussion on the modern use of the word *jongo* and its dimension as locus of enunciation in Brazil, see Paulo Dias, "O lugar da fala conversas entre o jongo brasileiro e o ondjango angolano," *Revista do Instituto de Estudos Brasileiros* 59 (2014): 329–67.

78 Edir Gandra, *Jongo da Serrinha: do terreiro aos palcos* (Rio de Janeiro: Giorgio Grafica e Editora, 1995).

79 Marcos André and Luciane Menezes, *Jongo do Quilombo São José* (Rio de Janeiro: Associação Brasil Mestiço, 2004).

80 Burns, *Nasci para sonhar e cantar*.

81 Ibid.

82 Nei Lopes, *O negro no Rio de Janeiro e sua tradição musical: partido-alto, calango, chula e outras cantorias* (Pallas, 1992), 68.

83 Kazadi Wa Mukuna, *Contribuição bantu na música popular brasileira* (Global Editora, 1978), 62.

84 Sodré, *Samba, O dono do corpo*.

85 Interview with the author in Portuguese and translated by the author.

Afterword

1 Gilberto Velho, *Autoria e criação artística*. Comunicação apresentada no colóquio "Artifícios e Artefactos: entre o literário e o antropológico." Fórum de Ciência e Cultura da UFRJ, RJ, September 9, 2004. Translated by the author.

Bibliography

Alberti, Verena, and Amílcar Araújo Pereira (eds.), *Histórias do movimento negro no Brasil: depoimentos ao CPDOC* (Rio de Janeiro: Pallas Editora, 2007).

Alberto, Paulina L., "When Rio was Black: Soul Music, National Culture, and the Politics of Racial Comparison in 1970s Brazil," *Hispanic American Historical Review* 89, no. 1 (2009): 3–39.

Albin, Ricardo Cravo, *MPB – A História de Um Século* (Rio de Janeiro: Funarte, 1998).

Alencar, Edigar de, *O carnaval carioca através da música* (Rio de Janeiro: Livraria Freitas Bastos, 1965).

Alencar, Edigar de, *Nosso Sinhô do Samba* (Rio de Janeiro: Funarte, 1981).

Andrade, Mário de, *Ensaio sobre a música brasileira* (São Paulo: Vila Rica; Brasília: INL, 1972). Available online at www.ufrgs.br/cdrom/mandrade/mandrade.pdf

André, Marcos, and Luciane Menezes, *Jongo do Quilombo São José* (Rio de Janeiro: Associação Brasil Mestiço, 2004).

Andrews, George Reid, *Blacks & Whites in São Paulo, Brazil, 1888–1988* (Madison, WI: University of Wisconsin Press, 1991).

Arinos, Afonso, *Obra completa* (Rio de Janeiro: Conselho Federal de Cultura, 1969).

Bacelar, Jefferson, and Maria Conceição B. de Souza, *O Rosário dos Pretos do Pelourinho* (Salvador: Fundação do Patrimônio Artístico e Cultural da Bahia, 1974).

Barr-Melej, Patrick, *Psychedelic Chile: Youth, Counterculture, and Politics on the Road to Socialism and Dictatorship* (Chapel Hill, NC: The University of North Carolina Press, 2017).

Bastide, Roger, *As religiões africanas no Brasil* (São Paulo: Pioneira/ USP, 1971).

Benjamin, Medea, and Maisa Mendonça, *Benedita da Silva: An Afro-Brazilian Woman's Story of Politics and Love* (Oakland: Food First Books, 1997).

Bergson, Henri, *La energia espiritual* (Madrid: Editora Espasa Calpe, 1996).

Bergson, Henri, *Matter and Memory* (New York: Zone Books, 1988).

Blanc, Aldir, Hugo Sukman, and Luiz Fernando Vianna, *Heranças do Samba* (Rio de Janeiro: Casa da Palavra, 2004).

Bobel, Chris, "'I'm Not an Activist, though I've Done a Lot of It:' Doing Activism, Being Activist and the 'Perfect Standard' in a Contemporary Movement," *Social Movement Studies* 6, no. 2 (2007): 147–59.

Bocskay, Stephen, "Undesired Presences: Samba, Improvisation, and Afro-politics in 1970s Brazil," *Latin American Research Review* 52, no. 31 (2007): 64–78.

Braga, Leandro, *Primeira Dama: A música de Dona Ivone Lara* (Rio de Janeiro: Gryphus, 2003).

Brito, Angela Neves-Xavier de. "Brazilian Women in Exile: The Quest for an Identity," *Latin American Perspectives* 13, no. 2 (1986): 58–80.

Browning, Barbara, *Samba: Resistance in Motion* (Bloomington, IN: Indiana University Press, 1995).

Burns, Mila, *Nasci para sonhar e cantar: Dona Ivone Lara — A mulher no samba* (Rio de Janeiro: Record, 2009).

Cabral, Sérgio, *As escolas de samba do Rio de Janeiro* (Rio de Janeiro: Editora Lumiar, 1996).

Cabral, Sérgio, "Getúlio Vargas e a música popular brasileira," *Ensaios de opinião* 2, nos. 2–1 (1975): 36–41.

Câmara, Yls Rabelo, "Sereia Amazônica, Iara e Yemanjá, entidades aquáticas femininas dentro do folclore das Águas no Brasil,"

Agália: Publicaçom internacional da Associaçom Galega da Lingua 97/98 (2009): 115–30.

Cardozo, Manoel S., "The Lay Brotherhoods of Colonial Bahia," *Catholic Historical Review* 33, no. 1 (1947): 12–30.

Carneiro, Edison, *Antologia do Negro Brasileiro* (Porto Alegre: Editora Globo, 1950).

Carneiro, Edison, *Candomblés da Bahia* (Salvador: Editora do Museu do Estado da Bahia, 1948).

Cascudo, Luís da Câmara, *Dicionário do Folclore Brasileiro* (Rio de Janeiro: Ed. Ediouro, 1954).

Castro, Ruy, *Chega de saudade: A história e as histórias da bossa-nova* (São Paulo: Companhia das Letras, 1990).

Cavalcanti, Maria Laura Viveiros de Castro, *Carnaval carioca: dos bastidores ao desfile* (Rio de Janeiro: Funarte; UFRJ, 1994).

Cavalcanti, Pedro Uchôa, Pedro Celso, and Jovelino Ramos (eds.), *Memórias do exílio, 1964/19??: De muitos caminhos, Vol. 1* (São Paulo: Livramento, 1978).

Collins, Patricia Hill, *On Intellectual Activism* (Philadelphia, PA: Temple University Press, 2013).

Costa, Albertina de Oliveira, Maria Teresa Porciúncula de Moraes, Norma Marzola, and Valentina da Rocha Lima (eds.), *Memórias das Mulheres do Exílio, Vol. 2* (Rio de Janeiro: Paz e Terra, 1980).

Costa, Emília Viotti da, *Da senzala à colônia* (São Paulo: Unesp, 1998).

Costa, Haroldo, *Salgueiro: Academia do Samba* (Rio de Janeiro: Record, 1984).

Costa, Luis Monteiro da, "A devoção de Nossa Senhora do Rosário na Cidade do Salvador," *Revista do Instituto Genealógico da Bahia* 10, no. 10 (1958): 95–113.

Covin, David, "Afrocentricity in O Movimento Negro Unificado," *Journal of Black Studies* 21, no. 2 (1990): 126–44.

Cunha, Maria Clementina Pereira, *Ecos da folia: Uma história social do carnaval carioca entre 1880 e 1920* (São Paulo: Editora Companhia das Letras, 2001).

Diamond, Irene, *Feminism and Foucault: Reflections on Resistance* (Lebanon, NH: Northeastern, 1988).

Dias, Paulo, "O lugar da fala conversas entre o jongo brasileiro e o ondjango angolano," *Revista do Instituto de Estudos Brasileiros* 59 (2014): 329–67.

Diniz, André, *Pixinguinha: O Gênio e o Tempo* (São Paulo: Casa da Palavra, 2012).

Diniz, André, and Diogo Cunha, *Na Passarela Do Samba* (São Paulo: Casa da Palavra, 2014).

Diniz, Edinha, *Chiquinha Gonzaga: uma história de vida* (Rio de Janeiro: Codecri, 1984).

Domingues, Petrônio, "Movimento Negro Brasileiro: alguns apontamentos históricos," *Tempo* 12, no. 23 (2007): 100–22.

Dunn, Christopher, *Brutality Garden: Tropicalia and the Emergence of a Brazilian Counterculture* (Chapel Hill, NC: The University of North Carolina Press, 2014).

Dunn, Christopher, *Contracultura* (Chapel Hill, NC: The University of North Carolina Press, 2016).

Efegê, Jota, *Ameno Resedá: O Rancho que foi Escola* (Rio de Janeiro: Editora Letras e Artes, 1965).

Efegê, Jota, *Figuras e coisas da música popular brasileira* (Rio de Janeiro: MEC/FUNARTE, 1979).

Farias, Edson, *O desfile e a Cidade. O carnaval espetáculo carioca* (Rio de Janeiro: e-papers, 2005).

Fausto, Boris, *A Revolução de 1930, Historiografia e História* (São Paulo: Companhia das Letras, 1997).

Fernandes, Dmitri Cerboncini, "A negra essencialização do samba," *Luso-Brazilian Review* 51–1 (2014): 132–56.

Fernandes, Florestan, *A integração do negro na sociedade de classes* (São Paulo: Editora Dominus/USP, 1965).

Fernandes, Florestan, and Roger Bastide, *Brancos e negros em São Paulo* (São Paulo: Cia. Editora Nacional, 1971).

Fernandes, Florestan, and Roger Bastide, *Capitalismo Dependente e Classes Sociais na América Latina* (Rio de Janeiro: Zahar, 1973).

Ferreira, Felipe, *O marquês e o jegue: estudo da fantasia para escolas de samba* (Rio de Janeiro: Altos da Glória, 1999).

Filho, Juvino Alves dos Santos, "Ensaio sobre o samba," *Repertório*, 43–46. Available online at www. revistarepertorioteatroedanca.tea.ufba.br/11/arq_pdf/ ensaiosobreosamba.pdf

Fontaine, Pierre-Michel (ed.), *Race, Class, and Power in Brazil* (Los Angeles, CA: Center for Afro-American Studies, UCLA, 1985).

Foucault, Michel, *The History of Sexuality, Volume 1: An Introduction* (New York, NY: Pantheon Books, 1978).

Freyre, Gilberto, *Casa-Grande e Senzala*, 50a edição revista (São Paulo: Global, 2005).

Freyre, Gilberto, *Sobrados e Mucambos*. 14a edição revista (São Paulo: Global, 2003).

Frostig, Karen, "Arts Activism: Praxis in Social Justice, Critical Discourse, and Radical Modes of Engagement," *Art Therapy* 28, no. 2 (2011): 50–56.

Furtado, Júnia Ferreira, *Chica da Silva: A Brazilian Slave of the Eighteenth Century* (New York, NY: Cambridge University Press, 2008).

Galinsky, Philip, "Co-option, Cultural Resistance, and Afro-Brazilian Identity: A History of the 'Pagode' Samba Movement in Rio de Janeiro," *Latin American Music Review / Revista de Música Latinoamericana* 17, no. 2 (Autumn–Winter, 1996): 120–49.

Gandra, Edir, *Jongo da Serrinha: do terreiro aos palcos* (Rio de Janeiro: Giorgio Grafica e Editora, 1995).

Gans, Herbert J., *Popular Culture and High Culture* (Nova York, NY: Basic Books Inc. Publishers, 1974).

Gessa, Marília, and Derek Pardue, *Racionais MCs' Sobrevivendo no Inferno* (New York, NY: Bloomsbury Academic, Forthcoming).

Gilroy, Paul, *The Black Atlantic: Modernity and Double Consciousness* (Cambridge, MA: Harvard University Press, 1993).

Gledhill, Sabrina, "Expandindo as margens do Atlântico Negro: Leituras sobre Booker T. Washington no Brasil," *Revista de História Comparada* 7, no. 2 (2013): 122–48.

Gomes, Rodrigo Cantos Savello, "Samba no feminino: transformações das relações de gênero no samba carioca nas três primeiras décadas do Século XX," Master's thesis, Universidade do Estado de Santa Catarina, Florianopolis, 2011. Available online at http://tede.udesc.br/handle/handle/1590

Gomes, Rodrigo Cantos Savello, "Tias Baianas que lavam, cozinham, dançam, cantam, tocam e compõem: um exame das relações de gênero no samba da Pequena África do Rio de Janeiro na primeira metade do século XX," Presentation, I Simpósio Brasileiro de Pós-Graduandos em Música XV Colóquio do Programa de Pós-Graduação em Música da UNIRIO, Rio de Janeiro, 2010.

Gonzalez, Lélia, "The Unified Black Movement: A New Stage in Black Political Mobilization," in *Race, Class, and Power in Brazil*, edited by Pierre-Michel Fontaine (Los Angeles, CA: UCLA, 1985), 120–34.

Grin, Monica, and Marcos Chor Maio, "O antirracismo da ordem no pensamento de Afonso Arinos de Melo Franco," *Topoi* 14, no. 26 (2013): 33–45.

Guimarães, Valéria, "A passeata contra a guitarra e a 'autêntica' música brasileira," in *Identidades brasileiras: composições e recomposições*, edited by Cristina Carneiro Rodrigues, Tania Regina de Luca, and Valéria Guimarães (São Paulo: Editora UNESP, 2014), 145–74.

Hanchard, Michael George, *Orpheus and Power: The Movimento Negro of Rio de Janeiro and São Paulo, Brazil, 1945–1988* (Princeton, NJ: Princeton University Press, 1994).

Hanchard, Michael George (ed.), *Racial Politics in Contemporary Brazil* (Durham, NC: Duke University Press, 1999).

Hentz, Isabel Cristina, and Ana Maria Veiga, "Entre o feminismo e a esquerda: contradições e embates da dupla militância," in *Resistências, Gênero e Feminismos contra as ditaduras no Cone Sul*, edited by Joana Maria Pedro, Cristina Scheibe Wolff, and Ana Maria Veiga (Florianópolis: Editora Mulheres, 2011), 145–64.

Hertzman, Marc A., *Making Samba: A New History of Race and Music in Brazil* (Durham, NC: Duke University Press, 2013).

Holanda, Sérgio Buarque de, *Roots of Brazil* (Notre Dame, IN: Notre Dame Press, 2012).

Horta, Bernardo Carneiro, *Nise: Arqueóloga dos Mares* (E+A Edições do Autor, 2008).

Jesus, Ilma Fátima de, "O pensamento do MNU–Movimento Negro Unificado," in *O pensamento negro em educação no Brasil: expressões do movimento negro* (São Carlos: UFSCar, 1997), 41–59.

Junior, Caio Prado, *Formação do Brasil contemporâneo* (São Paulo: Brasiliense, 1996).

Junior, Nilton Rodrigues, "Pastoras na Voz, Insubmissas na Vida? As mulheres da Velha Guarda da Portela," *Temiminós Revista Científica* 5, no. 1 (2015): 52–64.

Lapoujade, David, "The Normal and the Pathological in Bergson," *MLN* 120, no. 5 Comparative Literature Issue (2005): 1146–55.

Lopes, Nei, *O negro no Rio de Janeiro e sua tradição musical: partido-alto, calango, chula e outras cantorias* (Rio de Janeiro: Pallas, 1992).

Maggie, Yvonne, *Guerra de Orixá. Um estudo de ritual e conflito* (Rio de Janeiro: Jorge Zahar Editor, 2001).

Marques, Teresa Cristina Schneider, "Lembranças do exílio: as produções memorialísticas dos exilados pela ditadura militar brasileira," in *A construção da memória política*, org, Elias Medeiros and Naiara Molin (Pelotas-RS: UFPEL, 2011), 119–37.

Matta, Roberto da, *Carnavais, malandros e heróis: para uma sociologia do dilema brasileiro* (Rio de Janeiro: Rocco, 1979).

Matthias, Leon L, "Book Review: *Masters and Slaves*," *The American Catholic Sociological Review* 7, no. 4 (December 1946): 282–84.

Mello, Marcelo de, *O enredo do meu samba – a história de quinze sambas-enredo imortais* (Rio de Janeiro: Record, 2015).

Monteiro, Helene, "O ressurgimento do Movimento Negro no Rio de Janeiro na década de 70," Master's thesis, Universidade Federal do Rio de Janeiro, 1991.

Moura, Roberto, *Tia Ciata e a Pequena África no Rio de Janeiro* (Rio de Janeiro: Funarte, 1983).

Mukuna, Kazadi Wa, *Contribuição bantu na música popular brasileira* (São Paulo: Global Editora, 1978).

Mulvey, Patricia, "The Black Lay Brotherhoods of Colonial Brazil: A History," Ph.D. Dissertation, City University of New York, 1976.

Munhoz, Raquel, *Quelé, a voz da cor: Biografia de Clementina de Jesus* (Rio de Janeiro: Civilização Brasileira, 2017).

Nascimento, Abdias do, *O Genocídio do Negro Brasileiro* (Rio de Janeiro: Paz e Terra, 1978).

Nascimento, Abdias do, *O negro revoltado* (Rio de Janeiro: Editora Nova Fronteira, 1982).

Nascimento, Abdias do, "*Racial Democracy*" *in Brazil: Myth or Reality* (Ibadan: Sketch Publishers, 1977).

Nascimento, Abdias do, Paulo Freire, and Nelson Werneck Sodré (eds.), *Memórias do Exílio* (Lisboa: Arcádia, 1976).

Naves, Santuza Cambraia, *Da bossa nova à tropicália* (Rio de Janeiro: Zahar, 2001).

Naves, Santuza Cambraia, and Elizabeth Travassos, "O violão azul. Modernismo e música Popular," *DEBATES-Cadernos do Programa de Pós-Graduação em Música* 3 (2014): 97–101.

Neto, Lira, *Uma história do samba: Volume 1* (*As Origens*) (São Paulo: Companhia das Letras, 2017).

Neves, José Roberto Santos, *Maysa* (Vitória: Contexto Jornalismo e Assessoria Ltda/ Núcleo de projetos culturais e Ecológicos, 2004).

Nobile, Lucas, *Dona Ivone Lara: A Primeira-Dama do Samba* (Rio de Janeiro: Sonora Editora, 2015).

Oliveira, Aloysio de, *De Banda pra lua* (Rio de Janeiro: Editora Record, 1982).

Oliveira, Luciana Xavier de, "África Brasil (1976): uma análise midiática do album de Jorge Ben Jor," *Contemporanea-Revista de Comunicação e Cultura* 10, no. 1 (2012): 158–74.

Ott, Carlos, "A Irmandade do Nossa Senhora do Rosário dos Pretos do Pelourinho," *Afro-Ásia* 6–7 (1968): 119–26.

Peixoto, Luiz Felipe de Lima, and Zé Octavio Sebadelhe, *1976: Movimento Black Rio* (Rio de Janeiro: José Olympio, 2016).

Pereira, Amílcar Araújo, "Influências externas, circulação de referenciais e a constituição do movimento negro contemporâneo no Brasil: idas e vindas no 'Atlântico Negro,'" *Ciências e Letras* Porto Alegre, 44 (2008): 215–36.

Pereira, Amílcar Araújo, "Linhas (da cor) cruzadas: relações raciais, imprensa negra e Movimento Negro no Brasil e nos Estados

Unidos," in *O Movimento Negro Brasileiro: escritos sobre os sentidos de democracia e justiça social no Brasil*, edited by Amauri Mendes Pereira and Joselina da Silva (Belo Horizonte: Nandyala, 2009), 109–26.

Pimentel, João, *Jorge Aragão: O Enredo de um Samba* (Rio de Janeiro: Sonora Edições, 2016).

Pinho, Patricia de Santana, "Descentrando os Estados Unidos nos estudos sobre negritude no Brasil," *Revista Brasileira de Ciências Sociais* 20, no. 59 (2005): 37–50.

Pinto, Célia Regina Jardim, *Uma história do feminismo no Brasil* (São Paulo: Editora Fundação Perseu Abramo, 2003).

Pinto, L. A. Costa, *Recôncavo – Laboratório de Uma Experiência Humana* (Rio de Janeiro: Centro Latino-Americano de Pesquisas em Ciências Sociais, Publicação número 1, 1958).

Pickett, Brent L., "Foucault and the Politics of Resistance," *Polity* XXVIII, no. 4 (1996): 445–66.

Porciúncula, Paula Paraíso, "*A Dança da Solidão* (1972) e *Nervos de Aço* (1973): a arte nas capas de discos durante a ditadura no Brasil," TCC, Universidade Federal de Santa Catarina, 2016. Available online at: https://repositorio.ufsc.br/xmlui/bitstream/handle/123456789/179608/TCC_Paula_Paraiso_Porciuncula_2016_1.pdf?sequence=1&isAllowed=y.

Reginaldo, Lucilene, *Os rosários dos angolas – irmandades de africanos e crioulos na Bahia setecentista* (São Paulo: Alameda, 2011).

Reis, João José, "Identidade e diversidade étnicas nas irmandades negras no tempo da escravidão," *Tempo* 2, no. 3 (1996): 7–33.

Ribeiro, Alexandre Vieira, "Estimativas sobre o volume do tráfico Transatlântico de escravos para a Bahia, 1582–1851." Available online at http://anais.anpuh.org/wp-content/uploads/mp/pdf/ANPUH.S23.1078.pdf.

Ribeiro, Djamila, *O que é lugar de fala* (Belo Horizonte: Letramento, 2017).

Rio, João do, *As religiões no Rio* (1904). Available online at www.dominiopublico.gov.br/download/texto/bi000185.pdf

Rollemberg, Denise, *Exílio: Entre raízes e radars* (Rio de Janeiro: Record, 1999).

Saffioti, Heleieth, *A Mulher na Sociedade de Classes Mito e Realidade* (Petrópolis: Vozes, 1976).

Sandroni, Carlos, *Feitiço decente: transformações do samba no Rio de Janeiro (1917–1933)* (Rio de Janeiro: Jorge Zahar; Ed. UFRJ, 2001).

Sandroni, Carlos, *Samba de Roda do Recôncavo Baiano* (Instituto do Patrimônio Histórico e Artístico Nacional (IPHAN)). Available online at http://portal.iphan.gov.br/uploads/publicacao/PatImDos_SambaRodaReconcavoBaiano_m.pdf

Sansone, Livio, "Negritudes e racismos globais? Uma tentativa de relativizar alguns dos novos paradigmas 'universais' nos estudos da etnicidade a partir da realidade brasileira," *Horizontes Antropológicos* 4, no. 8 (1998): 227–37.

Santanna, Marilda, *As bambas do samba: mulher e poder na roda* (Salvador: Edfba, 2016).

Santos, Alexandre Reis dos, "Eu quero ver quando Zumbi chegar: negritude, política e relações raciais na obra de Jorge Ben (1963–1976)," M.A. thesis, History Department, Universidade Federal Fluminense, 2014.

Santos, Gislene Aparecida dos, *Mulher negra, homem branco. Um breve estudo do feminino negro* (Rio de Janeiro: Pallas, 2004).

Santos, Joel Rufino dos, "O movimento negro e a crise brasileira," *Politica e administração* 2, no. 2 (1985): 287–307.

Santos, Katia, *Ivone Lara: a dona da melodia* (Rio de Janeiro: Editora Garamond, 2010).

Santos, Katia Regina da Costa, *Dona Ivone Lara: Voz e Corpo da Síncopa do Samba*. Ph.D. Thesis, University of Georgia, 2005. Available at https://getd.libs.uga.edu/pdfs/santos_katia_c_200505_phd.pdf.

Santos, Thereza, "The black movement: without identity there is no consciousness or struggle," *UCLA Latin American studies*, 86, (1999): 23–30.

Schumaher, Schuma (ed.), *Dicionário mulheres do Brasil: de 1500 até a atualidade biográfico e ilustrado* (Rio de Janeiro: Jorge Zahar Editor, 2000).

Schütz, Alfred, *The Phenomenology of the Social World* (Evanston, IL: Northwestern University Press, 1967).

Scott, James C., *Domination and the Arts of Resistance: Hidden Transcripts* (New Haven, CT: Yale University Press, 2010).

Silva, Marília T. Barboza da, and Arthur L. de Oliveira Filho, *Silas de Oliveira, do jongo ao samba-enredo* (Rio de Janeiro: Funarte, 1981).

Skidmore, Thomas E., *Black into White: Race and Nationality in Brazilian Thought* (Durham, NC: Duke University Press, 1993).

Skidmore, Thomas E., *The Politics of Military Rule in Brazil, 1964–1985* (New York, NY: Oxford University Press, 1990).

Sodré, Muniz, *Samba, O dono do corpo* (Rio de Janeiro: Mauad, 1998).

Stanyek, Jason, and Fabio Oliveira, "Nuances of Continual Variation in the Brazilian Pagode Song 'Sorriso Aberto,'" in *Analytical and Cross-Cultural Studies in World Music*, edited by Michael Tenzer and John Roeder (New York, NY: Oxford University Press, 2011), 98–146.

Strauss, Anselm, *Espelhos e máscaras: a busca da identidade* (São Paulo: Edusp, 1999).

Tatit, Luiz, *O Século da Canção* (Cotia: Ateliê Editorial, 2004).

Teles, Amelinha, and Rosalina Santa Cruz Leite, *Da guerrilha à imprensa feminista: a construção do feminismo pós-luta armada no Brasil (1975–1980)* (São Paulo: Editora Intermeios, 2013).

Teles, Maria Amélia de Almeida, *Breve História do Feminismo no Brasil* (São Paulo: Editora Brasiliense, 1993).

Tinhorão, José Ramos, *História Social da Música Popular Brasileira* (São Paulo: Editora 34, 1998).

Tinhorão, José Ramos, *A Música Popular no Romance Brasileiro (vol II: séc XX [1a parte])* (São Paulo: Editora 34, 2000).

Tinhorão, José Ramos, *Pequena História da Música Popular. Segundo Seus Gêneros* (São Paulo: Editora 34, 2013).

Tinhorão, José Ramos, *O samba agora vai...* (Rio de Janeiro: J.C.M. Editores, 1969).

Twine, France Winddance, *Racism in a Racial Democracy: The Maintenance of White Supremacy in Brazil* (New Brunswick, NJ: Rutgers University Press, 1998).

Valença, Rachel, and Suetônio Valença, *Serra, Serrinha, Serrano, o império do samba* (Rio de Janeiro: Record, 2017).

Velho, Gilberto, *Individualismo e cultura: notas para uma antropologia da sociedade contemporânea* (Rio de Janeiro: Zahar, 1981).

Velho, Gilberto, *Projeto e Metamorfose: antropologia das sociedades complexas* (Rio de Janeiro: Jorge Zahar Editor, 1994).

Velho, Gilberto, and Karina Kushnir, *Autoria e criação artística* (Comunicação apresentada no colóquio "Artifícios e Artefactos: entre o literário e o antropológico." Fórum de Ciência e Cultura da UFRJ, RJ, 2004).

Velho, Gilberto, and Karina Kushnir, *Mediação, Cultura e política* (Rio de Janeiro: Aeroplano, 2001).

Velloso, Mônica Pimenta, "As tias baianas tomam conta do pedaço... Espaço e identidade cultural no Rio de Janeiro," *Estudos Históricos* 3, no. 6 (1990): 207–28.

Vianna, Hermano, "A meta mitológica da democracia racial," in *O Imperador das Idéias. Gilberto Freyre em questão*, edited by FALCÃO, Joaquim e ARAÚJO, Rosa Maria Barboza de (Rio de Janeiro: Fundação Roberto Marinho, 2001), 215–21.

Vianna, Hermano, *O Mistério do Samba* (Rio de Janeiro: Jorge Zahar Editor e Editora UFRJ, 1995).

Vicente, Eduardo, "Segmentação e consumo: a produção fonográfica brasileira −1965−1999," *ArtCultura*, Uberlândia 10, no. 16 (2008): 103−12. Available online at http://producao.usp.br/handle/BDPI/32361.

Vilhena, Luís Rodolfo, *Projeto e missão: o movimento folclórico brasileiro* (Rio de Janeiro: Funarte/ FGV, 1997).

White, John David, *The Analysis of Music* (Englewood Cliffs, NJ: Prentice-Hall, 1976).

Wodak, Ruth, *Discursive Construction of National Identity* (Edinburgh: Edinburgh University Press, 2009).

Audio and Visual

Candeia, "Sou mais Samba," in *Quatro Grandes do Samba* (Rio de Janeiro: RCA/BMG, 2001. CD, Track 7).

Chico Buarque de Hollanda, *Construção* (Rio de Janeiro: Marola Edições Musicais, 1971. LP).

Dona Ivone Lara, *Sorriso Negro* (Rio de Janeiro: WEA, 1982. LP).

Dona Ivone Lara, and Ile Aiyê. In the album *Rosário Dos Pretos – Cânticos*. Compilation, 1999. CD, Track 14.

Paulinho da Viola, *Nervos de Aço* (Rio de Janeiro: Odeon, 1973. LP).

Sambabook – Dona Ivone Lara. Compilation, Universal Music, 2015. DVD.

Uma noite em 67. Directed by Ricardo Calil and Renato Terra (Rio de Janeiro: VideoFilmes, 2010. DVD).

Index